"The Supremes"

Teaching Texts in Law and Politics

David A. Schultz
General Editor

Vol. 6

PETER LANG
New York • Washington, D.C./Baltimore • Boston • Bern
Frankfurt am Main • Berlin • Brussels • Vienna • Canterbury

Barbara A. Perry

"The Supremes"

Essays on the Current Justices
of the Supreme Court
of the United States

PETER LANG
New York • Washington, D.C./Baltimore • Boston • Bern
Frankfurt am Main • Berlin • Brussels • Vienna • Canterbury

Library of Congress Cataloging-in-Publication Data

Perry, Barbara A.
"The Supremes": essays on the current justices of the Supreme Court
of the United States / Barbara A. Perry.
p. cm. — (Teaching texts in law and politics; vol. 6)
Includes bibliographical references and index.
1. United States. Supreme Court Biography. 2. Judges—
United States Biography. I. Title. II. Series.
KF8744.P47   347.73'2634—dc21   99-33948
ISBN 0-8204-4046-9
ISSN 1083-3447

Die Deutsche Bibliothek-CIP-Einheitsaufnahme

Perry, Barbara A.:
"The supremes": essays on the current justices
of the Supreme Court of the United States / Barbara A. Perry.
–New York; Washington, D.C./Baltimore; Boston; Bern;
Frankfurt am Main; Berlin; Brussels; Vienna; Canterbury: Lang.
(Teaching texts in law and politics; Vol. 6)
ISBN 0-8204-4046-9

Cover design by Nona Reuter

Cover photo by Richard W. Strass, Smithsonian Institute

The paper in this book meets the guidelines for permanence and durability
of the Committee on Production Guidelines for Book Longevity
of the Council of Library Resources.

© 1999, 2001 Peter Lang Publishing, Inc., New York

Printed in the United States of America

For my godsons

Max Prinz

and

Jimmy Fowler

ACKNOWLEDGMENTS

In 1975, when I took my very first course in constitutional history with the late Mary Kay Tachau at the University of Louisville, she showed our class the famous 1968 CBS television interview that Justice Hugo Black had filmed with Martin Agronsky. From that moment, constitutional law, and the black-robed Supreme Court jurists who interpret it, captivated me. At the Smithsonian the next year, I saw on display Justice Black's judicial robe and the famous dog-eared copy of the Constitution that he always carried in his breast pocket. I excitedly wrote a postcard to Dr. Tachau telling her of my discovery as if I had seen the sacred relics of a revered saint.

It seemed as though I had reached nirvana when I interviewed most of the Court's members in the mid-1980s for my dissertation research. That experience was surpassed only by my year-long stint as a judicial fellow at the Supreme Court in 1994–95, where I had the chance to observe the justices frequently in oral argument and personal conversations. One of my duties as a fellow at the Court was to brief visiting dignitaries and students; inevitably they would ask about the ideologies, personalities, and biographies of the nine members of the tribunal. When I returned to the classroom at Sweet Briar College, I had a fresh store of observations on the justices to share with my own students. I am thankful to all of these groups who requested more information on the jurists of America's highest court for planting the seed that a brief reference source would be welcome on the subject.

I am particularly grateful to Owen Lancer who, while at Peter Lang Publishing, suggested the format for this text. His enthusiasm for the project spurred me to complete it in a timely fashion. His production assistant Benjamin Hallman guided me through several typesetting crises with expertise and encouragement, and he has earned my special thanks. As the series editor, Professor David Schultz offered his wise counsel and expertise on the Court.

Professor Henry Abraham's model of scholarship and perennially optimistic support were crucial to my bringing this study to fruition. Research assistants Christine Bump and Amy Campbell cheerfully and competently provided critical material at the outset of my undertaking. A Kenmore Grant from Sweet Briar College, made possible by the generosity of the Newman family, enabled me to complete this project. My extraordinary parents always knew when to ask, "Are you finished yet?" in such a way as to bolster my morale, and Mother added her superb proofreading skills to the enterprise. (Any remaining errors are my responsibility alone.) While she and my father always gave me hope for this present project, two special young gentlemen, Jimmy and Max, give me hope for the future.

TABLE OF CONTENTS

INTRODUCTION

The title of this book of essays on contemporary members of the Supreme Court of the United States will perhaps recall the popular Motown singing trio led by Diana Ross in the 1960s, but the title is meant to convey the obvious supremacy of the highest court in the land and the demonstrated merit of the members of the tribunal in the last decade of the twentieth century.

Most observers agree that the justices who currently occupy the black leather chairs behind the Supreme Court's mahogany bench are among the most capable to serve the tribunal since the Roosevelt Court in the 1940s. As of 1999, the Court's membership included, in order of seniority:

- William H. Rehnquist (appointed as associate justice by Richard Nixon in 1972; promoted to chief justice by Ronald Reagan in 1986);
- John Paul Stevens (nominated by Gerald Ford in 1975);
- Sandra Day O'Connor (nominated by Reagan in 1981);
- Antonin Scalia (nominated by Reagan in 1986);
- Anthony M. Kennedy (appointed by Reagan in 1988);
- David H. Souter (nominated by George Bush in 1990);
- Clarence Thomas (nominated by Bush in 1991);
- Ruth Bader Ginsburg (nominated by Bill Clinton in 1993);
- Stephen G. Breyer (nominated by Clinton in 1994).

Their educational backgrounds are superb. Rehnquist, O'Connor, Kennedy, and Breyer attended Stanford as undergraduates, and Rehnquist and O'Connor continued their law programs there. Souter was an undergraduate at Harvard; he, Scalia, Kennedy, and Breyer pursued their law degrees at its law school. Ruth Bader Ginsburg received her bachelor's degree from Cornell, studied law for two years at Harvard, and completed her law degree at Columbia after she moved to New York to be with her husband. Thomas and Scalia attended Catholic institutions for under-graduate studies—Holy Cross and Georgetown, respectively;

Thomas went on to Yale Law School. Stevens, with deep roots in the Windy City, attended the University of Chicago and Northwestern Law School. Two justices did postgraduate work at Oxford (Souter on a Rhodes Scholarship, Breyer on a Marshall Scholarship). Kennedy studied at the London School of Economics, and Rehnquist completed an M.A. in government at Harvard. Most would have been considered classic "overachievers," having received stellar grades and graduating at or near the top of their classes. Five were elected to Phi Beta Kappa as undergraduates (Rehnquist, Stevens, Kennedy, Souter, and Ginsburg); over half served on law reviews (Rehnquist, Stevens, O'Connor, Scalia, Ginsburg, and Breyer).

The nine justices also brought a range of political, governmental, and judicial experience to the Supreme Court. The Reagan administration (which appointed four of the nine current justices) placed a premium on previous court service, especially at the federal level, and succeeding presidents have also used that selection criterion. Rehnquist is the only member of the present Court to have ascended the bench without previous experience as a judge. (He had been a Supreme Court clerk, however, as had Stevens and Breyer.) Rehnquist served fourteen years as an associate justice before his promotion to chief. O'Connor and Souter possessed extensive state court experience, and the former had served in the Arizona Senate, including a stint as its majority leader. Kennedy, Ginsburg, and Breyer all had tenures of a dozen years or more on the U.S. circuit courts. Stevens and Scalia each spent five years on the federal appeals tribunals. Souter and Thomas had brief stints on the U.S. circuit benches just prior to their appointments to the Supreme Court. Experience in all three branches of the federal government before coming to the high court gives Justices Thomas and Breyer the edge in breadth of previous public service. Chief Justice Rehnquist possesses the most experience in private law practice (sixteen years), during which he was active in Republican party politics. He was assistant attorney general in the United States Department of Justice immediately prior to his elevation to the Supreme Court. Justice Thomas held two appointed positions in the federal government (at the Department of Education and the Equal Employment Opportunity Commission) before his first judgeship. Academe was Justice Ginsburg's proving ground for the federal bench, and Justices Kennedy and Breyer have taught extensively as adjunct professors. Scalia's résumé reflects a background of teaching law, executive-branch service, think-tank research, and private practice.

In its social characteristics, the Supreme Court of the late twentieth century can hardly be said to "look like America," but it is far more "representative" than in the past. Today's Court is unique in having two female members; and the "black seat," established in 1967 with Thurgood Marshall's appointment, remained intact (albeit controversial) with Clarence Thomas's 1991 nomination. For the first time in its history, a majority of the Court are members of minority religious groups: Kennedy, Scalia, and Thomas are Roman Catholic; Ginsburg and Breyer are Jewish. The other four members are Christian (O'Connor and Souter are Episcopalian, Rehnquist is Lutheran, and Stevens does not belong to any particular denomination). In geographic terms, this bench is top-heavy with Westerners and Northeasterners. O'Connor grew up near the Arizona–New Mexico border, and Kennedy and Breyer hail from northern California. Scalia and Ginsburg were raised in New York, and Souter is from New England. Rehnquist and Stevens hail from the Midwest, though the chief justice spent many years in a Phoenix law firm before coming to Washington. Clarence Thomas is the only Southerner on this Court. Of course, in some cases, careers and lifestyle choices have taken the justices far from their roots. In addition to maintaining a home in the Washington area, Rehnquist has a summer retreat in Vermont, Stevens spends considerable time in Florida, and Breyer had made his home near Boston for many years while serving on the First Circuit Court of Appeals. As of 1999, the average age of the justices was 65: Stevens was the oldest at 79, Rehnquist was 75, O'Connor 69, Ginsburg 66, Kennedy and Scalia 63, Breyer 61, Souter 60, and Thomas 51.

While most of the current justices came from middle- or upper-middle-class households and enjoyed numerous advantages in making their way up the educational and professional ladder, several overcame societal discrimination to achieve their positions on the nation's highest court. Justices O'Connor and Ginsburg faced gender-based handicaps at the outset of their careers. Although both graduated at or near the top of their law-school classes, neither was offered a prized Supreme Court clerkship, nor could either of them find an associate's position in private practice.

O'Connor finally launched her career through volunteer and public service, and Ginsburg became a law professor. Justice Thomas overcame a poverty-stricken early childhood to advance through Yale Law School's affirmative-action program, only to be denied a position in law firms; he began his career in the Missouri attorney general's office. Several members of the current Court have triumphed over personal tragedies and hardships. Sandra Day O'Connor is a breast cancer survivor; as a teenager, Ruth Bader Ginsburg lost her mother to cancer and then nursed her husband through testicular cancer while they both were in law school; Rehnquist was widowed in 1991 when his wife succumbed to cancer. Early in his career, Justice Kennedy's father died prematurely of a heart attack, and then Kennedy's mother, sister, and brother passed away in quick succession. Justice Thomas's father abandoned his family when Thomas was a young boy, and he and his brother were raised by their grandparents. Thomas and Stevens have endured divorces; both remarried.

In oral arguments, the current justices constitute one of the liveliest benches in recent memory. All but Thomas are frequent, persistent, and incisive questioners. Moreover, this Supreme Court contains some of the wittiest inquisitors the hallowed courtroom has ever witnessed. Increasingly, the sober, church-like atmosphere there is interrupted by laughter when Scalia delivers a sarcastic one-liner, Souter utters a droll quip in his New England accent, or Breyer presents a wry, professorial comment. With their rapier-like intellects and wits, these justices have made oral argument sessions unexpectedly entertaining, as well as edifying, events.

Jurisprudential and ideological labels are imprecise at best, but most observers agree on general categories and descriptions of the current justices' voting postures. From right to left on the political spectrum, Justices Scalia and Thomas are considered the most conservative, with the former committed to a text-based, originalist understanding of the Constitution. Chief Justice Rehnquist is a life-long conservative who pays considerable deference to federalism and the democratic legislative process. In the category of moderate-conservative "swing voters" are Justices Kennedy and O'Connor. Kennedy prides himself on his considered, sometimes agonizing, case-by-case approach to decisions.

Although O'Connor struggles to find the middle ground on vexing issues of race and abortion, she sides with the more liberal position in gender discrimination cases, but will often switch to a conservative stance in her votes favoring state governments. The most common voting alignment in narrowly decided rulings has recently consisted of Chief Justice Rehnquist and Justices O'Connor, Kennedy, Scalia, and Thomas.[1]

No liberals in the William Brennan or Thurgood Marshall image remain on the Court, but Justice Souter has begun following in the footsteps of his late friend Justice Brennan. Justices Souter, Stevens, Ginsburg, and Breyer sometimes side as a liberal bloc, and, if they can attract a fifth vote (usually O'Connor or Kennedy), will win the case. Although rulings on contentious cases draw the most publicity and tend to reflect a closely divided Court, the rate of unanimous decisions continues to grow—reaching over fifty percent in 1997–98.[2] Justices Ginsburg and Breyer are usually deemed moderate liberals for their reluctance to impose activist standards even when they reach a liberal decision. With his unique vision of the law, Justice Stevens's maverick approach repeatedly obliges him to write solo dissents or concurrences. His recently attained seniority, however, second only to Rehnquist, means that when the chief justice is in dissent and Stevens is in the majority, he can write the opinion for the Court himself. He has done so in the landmark cases striking down state term limits on members of Congress and ruling against President Clinton's claim of immunity from civil suits, such as the Paula Jones case. (*Clinton v. Jones* was a unanimous ruling; Chief Justice Rehnquist, a conservative Nixon and Reagan appointee, may have strategized that he should *not* write the decision against Clinton for fear of appearing too partisan. It is unlikely that the chief justice could have envisioned that he would eventually preside over Clinton's 1999 impeachment trial in the Senate.) Yet, generally, Stevens is so marginalized that he wrote only seven majority opinions in the 1997–98 term, compared to an average of over ten such opinions for the other eight justices.[3]

The impact of these seven appointees of Republican presidents and two appointees of a Democratic chief executive has been mixed on the nettlesome issues of the late twentieth century. The so-called Rehnquist Court has failed to roll back completely the precedents of the Warren and Burger eras. Abortion is still legal, with some limits on access to the procedure; organized, state-sponsored prayer in public schools remains unlawful; free-exercise-of-religion claims have been upheld but not if general secular laws impinge on those claims only incidentally; free speech and press continue to lie at the heart of American democracy; affirmative-action programs can exist but now must meet the highest level of judicial scrutiny; majority-minority voting districts are also subject to such strict analysis; gender classifications trigger a lower standard of scrutiny but generally have been nullified, except in the disparate treatment of males and females in the draft laws; gender preference has not been afforded protection under privacy rights or special status through the Fourteenth Amendment, but gays earned one victory even under the lowest level of Equal Protection Clause analysis; criminal rights have been diluted, especially in the search-and-seizure category, and death sentences are now more difficult to appeal from state to federal courts; indeed, national prerogatives, especially embodied in statutes passed under Congress's interstate commerce power, have generally been weakened to the benefit of state power (except in a few instances such as state term limits on members of Congress); and the office of the presidency has not fared well, with invalidation of the line-item veto, upholding of the independent-counsel statute, and rejection of presidential immunity from civil suits.

Although its docket has shrunk by nearly half over the last decade for a variety of reasons,[4] the Supreme Court remains the jewel in the crown of the American governmental system. Indeed, it is the envy of judiciaries worldwide for its leadership of an independent judicial branch, for the professionalism and integrity of its members, and for the dignity of its public procedures and symbolism. Not surprisingly, it consistently scores higher than Congress or the presidency in polls measuring public confidence in governmental institutions. As Justice David Souter describes the Supreme Court's exalted status in the American polity: "Most people are willing to accept the fact that the Court tries to play it straight. That acceptance has been built up by the preceding hundred justices . . . going back to the beginning. We are, in fact, trading on the good faith and the conscientiousness of the justices who went before us. The power of the Court is the power of trust earned—the trust of the American people."[5]

ENDNOTES

1. Joan Biskupic, "Balance of Power," *Washington Post*, July 3, 1998, p. A17.
2. Frank J. Murray, "Decisions Don't Give Court Clear Identity," *Washington Times*, June 29, 1998, p. A1.
3. Ibid., p. A7.
4. These include removal of mandatory jurisdiction cases from the Court's docket by Congress in the late 1980s, uniformity of decisions in a federal judiciary guided by twelve-years' worth of Reagan/Bush appointees, and a more conservative Court less willing to use the law to pursue a social agenda. See David M. O'Brien's "The Rehnquist Court's Shrinking Plenary Docket," *Judicature* 81 (September-October 1997): 58–65.
5. Qtd. in York Associates Television, Inc. (producer), *The Supreme Court of the United States* (Washington: Supreme Court Historical Society, 1997), video.

CHAPTER ONE

William H. Rehnquist

On January 17, 1995, Chief Justice William H. Rehnquist emerged from behind the red velvet curtains to ascend the bench of the U.S. Supreme Court and take his seat in the center chair. He had performed this ritual for almost nine years since his promotion to chief justice in 1986, but that day in January 1995 was different. "The Chief" prompted twitters and craned necks from the audience. The source of the whispers and stares among the visitors was a set of four metallic gold stripes affixed to each arm of his black robe. At an institution where tradition, precedent, and the "cult of the robe" reign supreme, the chief's alterations to this judicial garb resulted in a flood of media comment. All of the major newspapers reported the story, which spread throughout the country on the wire services. Rehnquist confirmed that his new customized robe was patterned after the lord chancellor's costume in the Gilbert and Sullivan operetta *Iolanthe*. He had seen a production of the play and admired the robe's distinctive markings. The alteration reflects several aspects of the chief justice's personality. He loves musical theater, especially Gilbert and Sullivan; has a whimsical sense of humor; and obviously feels completely confident in his role as the preeminent jurist in the United States, but is not beyond self-deprecation.

William Rehnquist (his surname means "mountain goat" in Swedish) is of Nordic stock. He is tall and sturdy, although a bit stooped owing to a bad back and his septuagenarian status. In his youth, with a full head of hair, he was boyishly handsome, with a sparkling smile. He was born on October 1, 1924, to William Benjamin and Margery Peck Rehnquist. His father, a first-generation Swedish American and paper salesman, did not attend college, but his mother was a graduate of the University of Wisconsin, where she majored in French. With her fluency in five languages, she worked as a translator for export companies in Milwaukee. Some say that the chief justice inherited his brilliance from his mother.

Young Bill and his sister, Jean, grew up in a wealthy suburb of Milwaukee, called Shorewood, in a home that their parents had bought new in 1923 shortly after their marriage. The community was unabashedly Republican in the midst of the Great Depression and FDR's New Deal. The latter was disparaged at every opportunity, and Republican leaders like Herbert Hoover, Alf Landon, and Wendell Wilkie (albeit losers in presidential politics) were lionized. Rehnquist's father was a conservative among conservatives and advocated his political views with vigor. In later years, he would rail against the welfare state. Ironically, the Rehnquists lost their house to foreclosure in 1939, and the family subsequently rented a series of houses.

The future chief justice attended public schools in Shorewood, where he was noted for his keen intellect, ability to quote Shakespeare and Winston Churchill, and encyclopedic knowledge of history. But he was not a grind; one of his close friends from the teen years recalls, "He was always phenomenal at school, and I can never remember him studying."[1] Early on, his conservatism was much in evidence. When one of his elementary-school teachers asked him what he wanted to do when he grew up, he responded, "I'm going to change the government."[2] In high school his sense of humor revealed itself in a tongue-in-cheek school newspaper column he co-wrote and signed, "Boreign Correspondents."

Rehnquist graduated from high school in 1941, the summer before Pearl Harbor, and won a scholarship to Kenyon College, an all-male liberal arts institution in Gambier, Ohio. Although it had a fine reputation, it was small and isolated, and Rehnquist found the atmosphere not to his liking. He left after one quarter and joined the Army Air Corps as a weather observer. During his three-year hitch, he rose to the rank of sergeant and completed his tour of duty in North Africa. Photos of his last posting show him riding a camel.

Like numerous other veterans who had postponed higher education for service in World War II, Rehnquist enrolled in college on the G.I. Bill. This time he entered Stanford University and found the intellectual environment more suitable. He was elected to Phi Beta Kappa upon his graduation in 1948 with bachelor's and master's degrees in political science. During these years, Friedrick Hayek's book *The Road to Serfdom*, which argued against the welfare state, made a profound impression on the future justice. The study's thesis jibed perfectly with Rehnquist's early philosophy of government and economics. He decided to pursue another master's degree in political science, this time at Harvard. Not surprisingly, the left-leaning Ivy League campus galled him, and he escaped Harvard liberalism by returning to Stanford to pursue a law degree. He had earned a scholarship there with a score of 99.6 on the law school entrance exam.

Rehnquist's razor-sharp intellect was perfectly suited to the Socratic method. One of his fellow students recollects, "He obviously was a complete standout. When the professors got through abusing everybody and wanted the right answer, they would call on Bill."[3] His classmate, Sandra Day, who as Mrs. O'Connor would one day join him on the Supreme Court, attests to his intellectual superiority in law school. They both served as editors on the law review and graduated in 1952 with elections to the law honor society, the Order of the Coif. They even dated for a while before they each found different mates. Rehnquist married Natalie Cornell of San Diego in August 1953.

Between graduation from law school and marriage, however, Rehnquist held the most prestigious postgraduate position a new lawyer can attain. While now virtually all Supreme Court law clerks serve one year on a lower federal court before assuming their jobs at the high tribunal, in the 1950s justices accepted newly minted law grads. While visiting Stanford to dedicate a building, Justice Robert H. Jackson interviewed Rehnquist, who had been recommended by one of his professors, an ex-Jackson clerk himself. The future justice tried to bone up on his constitutional law, but then decided that tactic was futile. He found Justice Jackson to be a very pleasant interviewer; they spent little time discussing substantive matters, however, so Rehnquist thought he had failed to secure the plum clerkship. To his surprise, he received an offer from Jackson in the fall of 1951 and was able to start in February 1952 after his mid-year graduation.

Rehnquist's own description of his first day on the job is vivid. He remembers his self-doubt over arriving halfway through the term, while all the other clerks had been on board since its beginning in October. He even despaired over his typing skills. Initially, he was fraught with concern over whether he had the expertise and wisdom to make the right recommendation to Justice Jackson regarding *certiorari* petitions. As a clerk, he was assigned to read a portion of the cases that had been appealed to the Supreme Court and make a determination on whether the case should be accepted. On his initial day, mulling over the first petition, he was tempted to put it aside until he felt more confident. Then he asked himself, "When will I know more than I do now?" As the chief justice notes, "Perhaps it is just my own way of working, but I have always preferred where possible to go through one thing from beginning to end, do what I had to do with it, and move on to the next thing."[4] To this day, that is how Rehnquist has approached his work on the Court. By his own account, his clerkship with Justice Jackson was a rewarding experience, but he later publicly criticized his fellow clerks for betraying an ideology that he described as "to the 'left' of either the nation or the Court." He also accused the majority of clerks of displaying "extreme solicitude for the claims of Communists and other criminal defendants, expansion of federal power at the expense of State power, [and] great sympathy toward any government regulation of business."[5]

Like all ex-Supreme Court clerks, Rehnquist could have had his pick of associate positions in top East or West Coast law firms, making what was then considered the princely sum of $700 a month. But quality of life has always been a chief priority for him, and he chose to go to a Phoenix law firm, Cunningham, Carson & Messinger, where the pressure would be less severe and the city a pleasant place to raise a family. Between 1955 and 1959, the Rehnquists had three children, James, Janet, and Nancy. He now enjoys telling the amusing story of how he attempted to persuade Cunningham, Carson to raise his starting salary of $300 per month by $50 in light of what he could have earned in New York or Los Angeles, but the Phoenix firm would not budge. He stayed with them for several years before hanging out a shingle with another attorney. Ultimately, Rehnquist practiced law for sixteen years in Phoenix, with a primary emphasis on civil litigation. He was also active in Arizona's Republican Party, including the presidential campaigns of Barry Goldwater and Richard Nixon. He met and impressed Richard Kleindienst, who would become attorney general in Nixon's cabinet. The contact paid off when Attorney General Kleindienst recommended Rehnquist for the position of assistant attorney general in the Department of Justice's Office of Legal Counsel. He began the job at the start of the first Nixon administration in January 1969 and would henceforth make the Washington area his home.

At the Justice Department, Rehnquist established a visible role for himself defending the Nixon administration's legal policies before Congress. Not surprisingly, Rehnquist supported such conservative efforts as increased government wiretapping and surveillance of Americans (at the height of the anti-Vietnam War protests and the civil rights movement) and tightened limits on materials defined as obscene. Even members of Congress who disagreed with these measures found Rehnquist's defense of them to be cogent and articulate. He also argued a case before the U.S. Supreme Court in 1970, and continues to use the experience as a basis for offering advice to lawyers who might someday appear before the Court over which he now presides.

Another major duty of the assistant attorney general was the screening of possible nominees to the U.S. Supreme Court. Early on, the Nixon administration experienced a flurry of appointments to the high bench. Nixon had named Warren Burger to the chief justiceship in 1969 and Harry Blackmun to an associate's seat in 1970 (after the Senate rejected his first two nominees for the position, Clement F. Haynsworth, Jr. and G. Harold Carswell, Jr.). Within six days in September 1971, two more justices (Hugo Black and John Marshall Harlan II) retired from the Court. Eventually, Rehnquist was told not to attend any more meetings of the screening committee at the Department of Justice—a sure sign that he was under consideration. Indeed he was, but apparently not as Nixon's first choice for the Harlan vacancy. Evidence obtained from taped Nixon conversations, as revealed in a 1998 trial over payment to the late president's estate for records the government seized from him in 1974, indicates that then-Senator Howard Baker, Jr. (R.-Tenn.) was the preferred nominee. Attorney General John Mitchell notified Baker, who had little interest in moving across the street from Congress to the third branch. While the senator from Tennessee mulled over the possible appointment at the Supreme Court with his friend Justice Potter Stewart, the administration decided to move on to someone else—a man Nixon mistakenly called "Renchberg" and "Renchquist."

Many years later, Rehnquist chuckled over President Nixon's mangling of the Swedish surname. In retrospect, Rehnquist was not surprised that the president only knew that his name began with an R. After all, the assistant attorney general served in a sub-Cabinet-level position in which he had met with Nixon only twice. As a law clerk, Rehnquist had briefly encountered Vice President Nixon while dating his secretary. In the 1960 presidential campaign, Rehnquist secured hotel rooms for the Nixon campaign and met the entourage at the Phoenix airport. It was thus Rehnquist's loyal and competent service to the Nixon administration and his influential contacts in the Justice Department, rather than a close working relationship with the president, that led to Rehnquist's nomination to the high court. With just forty-eight-hours notice, the forty-seven-year-old Arizonan was nominated to the Supreme Court on October 21, 1971. (One day later, Nixon nominated Lewis F. Powell, Jr. to the seat vacated by Justice Black.) In presenting Rehnquist to the national television audience, Nixon praised him as a "guardian of our Constitution . . . the president's lawyer's lawyer . . . [and] outstanding in every intellectual endeavor he has ever undertaken."[6]

Rehnquist has noted that his nomination was probably "sealed" by his Supreme Court clerkship with Justice Jackson.[7] It also precipitated a major controversy in the Senate's consideration of him. A memo, drafted by Rehnquist and discovered in Jackson's *Brown v. Board of Education* file, argued for maintenance of the "separate but equal" doctrine, the Supreme Court's 1896 creation validating racial segregation. The Rehnquist memo concluded that the Court should not void segregated public schools that were being challenged in the *Brown* litigation. When questioned about the memo in 1971, Rehnquist explained that he had merely outlined Jackson's own views on *Brown* when the justice requested such a précis for use in an upcoming conference with his colleagues. Although many senators were skeptical about Rehnquist's explanation of the memo, as well as his relative youth, lack of judicial experience, and consistent support of conservative causes, the Senate confirmed his nomination on December 10, 1971, by a vote of 68–26. He took the oath of office and joined the Supreme Court, along with Justice Powell, just after New Year's Day in 1972.

In a tribute to his colleague Lewis Powell, who retired from the Court in 1986, Rehnquist explained that as judges "[e]ach one of us brings to the bench a mind imprinted with previous experience, and that experience undoubtedly influences, to a certain extent, how we go about the process of deciding cases."[8] Yet Rehnquist concluded that the traditional process of judging mitigates judges' "individual predilections in any given case. Judging has a large individual component in it, but the individual contribution of a good judge is filtered through the deliberative process of the court as a body. . . ."[9]

Although Rehnquist's argument may have validity in any particular case, his own conservative views are readily apparent in the body of cases in which he has participated in more than a quarter-century on the Supreme Court. Whether writing for the majority or dissenting alone, Rehnquist has espoused widely recognized conservative viewpoints through his deference to government over individual rights, respect for legislative actions in contrast to judicial fiat, and faith in the constitutional drafters' intentions, especially regarding federalism. In his early years on the Court, for example, he publicly rejected the "living Constitution" jurisprudence advocated by his colleague Justice Brennan as a way of updating the U.S. Constitution, via judicial interpretation, to recognize modern views of human dignity. Instead, Rehnquist declared that representative government required constitutional revision through majoritarian movements that prevailed upon elected representatives (not appointed judges) to embody such changes in positive law. Article V in the Constitution provided for just such constitutional change through the amendment process.

In one of his most enduringly visible dissents, Justice Rehnquist was on the losing side with Justice Byron White in the 7–2 *Roe v. Wade* decision, handed down just one year after Rehnquist ascended the bench. His dissenting opinion reflects a deference to constitutional language by noting that the Court had invalidly discovered a right to abortion in the Fourteenth Amendment that was nowhere contemplated by the framers of that 1868 change in the Constitution.

Rehnquist was also in dissent in a 1979 statutory interpretation case in which Justice Brennan determined for the Court that, despite the letter of the law in the 1964 Civil Rights Act banning racial discrimination in employment, the "spirit" of the statute condoned affirmative action. Rehnquist's enraged dissent from Brennan's majority opinion in *United Steelworkers of America v. Weber*, in which the Court ruled against Weber's claim of reverse discrimination, excoriated the decision as analogous to the famous magician Harry Houdini's sleight of hand. Rehnquist, who had also voted against the University of California at Davis Medical School's affirmative-action plan in the 1978 landmark *Bakke* decision, concluded that the Court's ruling in *Weber* "introduce[d] . . . a tolerance for the very evil that the law was intended to eradicate, without offering even a clue as to what the limits on that tolerance may be. . . . The Court has sown the wind. Later courts will face the impossible task of reaping the whirlwind."[10]

In sex discrimination cases, Rehnquist has been reluctant to apply expanded equal-protection analysis under the Fourteenth Amendment to gender-based laws and public policy. He was once more in dissent in *Frontiero v. Richardson* (when the Court struck down in 1973 a federal law that automatically qualified male service personnel for spousal benefits but that required female personnel to show proof of dependency) and in *Craig v. Boren* (when three years later the Court invalidated an Oklahoma statute prohibiting sale of 3.2 percent beer to males under twenty-one but to females only under eighteen). In *Frontiero* Rehnquist's dissent was solo, such a frequent occurrence that his clerks admiringly dubbed him the "Lone Ranger" and presented him with a doll portraying the erstwhile cowboy hero, which the justice proudly displayed in his chambers. Harvard Law Professor Laurence Tribe, a former Brennan clerk and advocate for liberal causes, conceded that "[e]ven in lone dissent, [Rehnquist] has helped define a new range of what is possible."[11]

In a 1980 lecture at the University of Arizona, Rehnquist defended the role of dissenting justices in the judicial process, arguing, "I simply do not think that one who reflects upon the wide range of issues which parties seek to litigate in courts today would conclude that unanimity of decision in every case is either a feasible or desirable goal."[12] Never permanently consigned to the minority, he wrote the majority opinion in the 1981 *Rostker v. Goldberg* case, in which he upheld for a 6–3 Court the Draft Registration Act of 1980 and its applicability only to males. As chief justice, though, Rehnquist departed from this consistent path in gender cases to join the Court's seven-person majority in the 1996 VMI Case, striking down the state-funded military academy's policy that banned females from enrolling. He contributed a concurrence that was narrower in its reasoning than Justice Ruth Bader Ginsburg's majority opinion.

Rehnquist's death-penalty jurisprudence exemplifies both his deference to government over individual rights and his confidence in legislative mandates, especially at the state level. In his first term on the Supreme Court, he dissented from the majority's view (albeit a splintered one expressed in an unusual *per curiam* judgment, with all nine justices filing separate opinions) that the death penalty as then carried out constituted cruel and unusual punishment in violation of the Eighth Amendment. Rehnquist urged in his dissent from the decision in *Furman v. Georgia* that democratic self-government, which had enacted death-penalty statutes in various states of the Union, was just as important as individual criminal rights. He was with the majority four years later when the Court reinstated the death penalty in *Gregg v. Georgia*. During his tenure as chief justice, Rehnquist has solidified and led a majority faction on the Court to limit state death penalty appeals in federal courts. In the 1993 case of *Herrera v. Collins*, he wrote for a six-person majority ruling that condemned prisoners who have exhausted their appeals and then produce new evidence that could prove their innocence have no right to be heard by a federal court. He also led the Court's sanctioning of the 1996 Antiterrorism and Effective Death Penalty Act, which imposed stringent limits on any federal court's consideration of a second or additional *habeas corpus* petition from a state convict. (The petition of *habeas corpus*, meaning literally "you have the body" in Latin, has become a procedural lifeline for death-row inmates, who use it to delay their executions.)[13]

Rehnquist's initial breakthrough victory in his crusade to right the balance between federal government and state and local governments came in the 1976 case of *National League of Cities v. Usery*, which struck down the Fair Labor Standards Act's application of federal wage and hour regulations to state employees. The Rehnquist-authored majority opinion for a narrowly split Court breathed life into the dormant Tenth Amendment, which reserves to the states powers not explicitly granted to the federal government or explicitly denied to the states. The *Usery* landmark was short-lived, however, as the Court overruled itself in 1985's *Garcia v. San Antonio Metropolitan Transit Authority*. Justice Blackmun facilitated the overturning of precedent by switching to the federal government's side, which he had eschewed in *Usery*. The Court vindicated Rehnquist's pro-federalism and pro-state posture in 1995 with its invalidation of the Gun-Free School Zones Act in *U.S. v. Lopez*. Chief Justice Rehnquist's majority opinion held that Congress had overstepped its interstate commerce power by enacting the anti-gun-possession law. He also happily joined the Scalia-led majority that struck down the "unfunded mandates" of the Brady Handgun Act, requiring states to monitor enforcement provisions of the congressional gun-control statute.

Although sitting Supreme Court justices are usually disinclined to comment publicly on laws that could come before them in the future, Rehnquist has challenged the wisdom of statutes such as the Violent Crime Control and Law Enforcement Act of 1994. The chief justice recognizes that Congress was responding to public outcries against violent criminal activity, but he is adamantly opposed to the "federalization" of criminal law, which creates federal offenses out of those acts that previously were addressed only by state criminal statutes. As Rehnquist concluded in an attack on the 1994 Crime Bill, "It remains for those of us who strongly believe in federalism—that the historic division between the proper business of the state courts and the proper business of the federal courts should be respected unless there is good reason to do otherwise—to work hard to see that the state courts do the best possible job of enforcing the laws presently on the books."[14]

Rehnquist has also crusaded on the Court for more government accommodation of religious claims in church-state cases. He was thus in dissent in *Stone v. Graham* (the 1981 decision banning a law that required the posting of the Ten Commandments in Kentucky public schools) and in *Wallace v. Jaffree* (the 1985 case invalidating a state-sponsored "moment of silence" for "meditation or voluntary prayer" in Alabama's school system). In the free-exercise-of-religion realm, Rehnquist authored a cogent analysis of the modern tension between the First Amendment's two religion clauses in his dissent from the 1981 ruling in *Thomas v. Review Board of the Indiana Employment Security Division*. He blamed the social-welfare state, application of the Bill of Rights to the states, and broad judicial interpretation of both religion clauses (none of which the framers of the First Amendment could have anticipated) for the clash between religion and government. As chief justice, Rehnquist led the 5–4 Court in *Zobrest v. Catalina School District*, a 1993 case allowing the use of public funds to pay for a sign-language interpreter to accompany a deaf child to a parochial school. The decision marked the first time a public employee was, in effect, allowed to be part of a religious school's instructional program.

Rehnquist has served as chief justice since Ronald Reagan promoted him to the Court's center chair in 1986. (He is only the third justice to be elevated directly from associate to chief; Harlan Fiske Stone and Edward White were the other two.) On June 17, 1986, then-Chief Justice Warren E. Burger made a surprise announcement that he would resign from the Court to supervise the Bicentennial of the United States Constitution in 1987. President Reagan immediately nominated Associate Justice Rehnquist to replace the seventy-nine-year-old Burger, and named U.S. Circuit Court Judge Antonin Scalia to the vacated Rehnquist seat on the high court. To move from the title "Lone Ranger" to "chief justice" in a little over fourteen years represented a victory for Rehnquist and the conservative movement led by the Reagan administration.

When Rehnquist's hearings began before the Republican-controlled Senate Judiciary Committee at the end of July 1986, he made no apologies for his demonstrated conservative record on the bench and offered no hope to his critics that he would undergo an ideological conversion once installed in the Court's center chair. His most vociferous opponent, Senator Edward M. Kennedy (D.-Mass.), bolstered by support from Professor Laurence Tribe, assailed Rehnquist's "record of massive isolated dissent," concluding that he was "too extreme on race, too extreme on women's rights, too extreme on freedom of speech, too extreme on separation of church and state, too extreme to be chief justice."[15] Sen. Kennedy's tirade was indicative of the bitterness that would mark the debate over Rehnquist's promotion. Critics scoured his personal and professional record for any shred of evidence that might derail the nomination. The memo supporting racial segregation, which Rehnquist had written during his clerkship under Justice Jackson, resurfaced; this time Rehnquist's allegedly racist views were buttressed by the revelation that the deeds to his homes in Phoenix and Vermont contained racially restrictive covenants. He was also accused of harassing black voters during the 1950s and '60s while he was a Republican party official in Phoenix. Even his brother-in-law came forward to allege that Rehnquist had mishandled a family trust.

Nevertheless, the Judiciary Committee voted 13–5 on August 14 to recommend his nomination to the full Senate. The GOP majority in the upper house of Congress (ushered in on the coattails of Reagan's impressive win over Jimmy Carter in the 1980 presidential election) was decisive in Rehnquist's ultimate victory. After another month of bruising debate, on September 17 the Senate voted 65–33 to confirm William Hubbs Rehnquist as the sixteenth chief justice of the United States. The thirty-three negative votes represented the largest number of "nays" ever cast against a nominee who won confirmation. The day after his confirmation, Rehnquist made a rare appearance before journalists on the front plaza of the Supreme Court for a brief press conference. Described by the *Washington Post* as "characteristically amiable and acting for all the world as if nothing had happened," the newly confirmed chief justice predictably commented that he was glad the process had "run its course."[16] He was neither bitter nor smug in his reaction to the grueling battle that preceded his triumph.

On September 26, 1986, just a few days short of his sixty-second birthday, Rehnquist took two oaths of office (one at the White House and one at the Supreme Court), both administered by his immediate predecessor Chief Justice Burger. The Burger era was now officially history, and the Rehnquist Court was in place, with its most junior justice, Antonin Scalia, also sworn in on the 26th, in Rehnquist's vacated associate position.

As early as 1980, Rehnquist had made public some of his musings regarding the chief justice's role: "As long as the 220-odd million inhabitants of this country see fit to confide the 'judicial power of the United States' to 'one Supreme Court,' it is surely best that it be a collegiate court which no Chief Justice needs to, or is capable of, 'dominating' or even of 'harmonizing' by virtue of his very limited special prerogatives as compared to those of his eight colleagues."[17] Even from ideological opponents on the Court, Rehnquist received high praise for his effective and affable leadership; the late Justice Brennan, before his 1990 retirement from the bench, categorized Rehnquist as "the most all-around successful" of the three chief justices under whom he had served.[18] (Earl Warren and Warren Burger were the other two.) Rehnquist runs a tight ship in private conferences with his colleagues, reportedly letting them speak their minds but keeping the discussion of cases on a narrow course. In public oral-argument sessions he is a dour presider, forcing counsel to stay directly on point and occasionally declaring, "The spectators are admonished to remain silent while the Court is in session!" He once vehemently chastised an attorney for giving opposite answers to the same question posed by two different justices. When the floundering lawyer apologetically said he did not mean "to confuse the Court," Rehnquist retorted, "You haven't so much confused us as just made us gravely wonder . . . how well-prepared you are for this argument." As the attorney sputtered, Rehnquist icily interrupted, "Your time has expired." The counsel, who not surprisingly went on to lose his case 9–0, later told a reporter, after Rehnquist's scathing treatment, "I felt like I dropped out of a tall cow's ass."[19]

Until his retirement in 1990, Justice Brennan used his formidable intellect and charm to marshal the five votes needed to achieve a victory for the liberal causes he championed during his thirty-four-year tenure on the high court. Chief Justice Rehnquist continued to play his previous role of dissenting when the case required a break from Brennan's expansive constitutional interpretation. In *Texas v. Johnson*, for example, Brennan wrote for the five-person majority (which he had persuaded Justices Scalia and Kennedy to join) that flag-burning as a form of political protest was protected expression under the First Amendment. The chief justice penned a bitter dissent, emphasizing the over 200-year history of the American flag's "unique position as the symbol of our Nation" and the fact that "millions of Americans regard it with an almost mystical reverence." Rehnquist argued that while "the Court's role as the final expositor of the Constitution is well established . . . its role as a platonic guardian . . . has no place in our system of government."[20] He would have deferred to the Texas legislature's right to follow public opinion and protect the flag from desecration.

Occasionally, however, Rehnquist surprised longtime Court observers with an unpredictable vote or opinion authorship. He wrote the Court's decisions in *Meritor Savings Bank v. Vinson* (the 1986 sex discrimination claim resolved in the plaintiff's favor), *Hustler Magazine v. Falwell* (the Rev. Falwell's unsuccessful 1987 libel and emotional-distress suit against Larry Flynt's magazine for a crude ad parody of the Moral Majority's leader), and *Morrison v. Olson* (the case rejecting the 1988 challenge to the independent counsel/special prosecutor law).

Yet in the 1990s, Rehnquist's leadership of a conservative faction on the Court helped to produce landmark rulings in cases challenging affirmative action (*Adarand v. Peña*), restricting Congress's commerce power (*U.S. v. Lopez*), limiting federal judicial power in school desegregation (*Missouri v. Jenkins II*), restraining death-penalty appeals from state to federal courts (*Felker v. Turpin* and *Herrera v. Collins*), reducing the number of "majority-minority" voting districts (*Shaw v. Hunt*), and elevating property rights to a higher plane of protection (*Dolan v. City of Tigard*). Neither Rehnquist nor his conservative colleagues on the Court, however, have succeeded in eliminating the right to abortion on demand or completely dismantling the wall of separation between church and state established by previous Courts.

In 1997–98 the Supreme Court was split 5–4 in fifteen cases out of the ninety-one signed rulings. The most frequent winning alliance in these narrowly decided rulings was Rehnquist, O'Connor, Kennedy, Scalia, and Thomas.[21] On a poignant note, the chief justice, who lost his wife in 1991 after a long battle with cancer, wrote for a unanimous Court in two 1997 cases (*Washington v. Glucksberg* and *Vacco v. Quill*) that there is no constitutional right to physician-assisted suicide. "The Chief," as Court employees refer to their boss, has remained a widower. For several years after his wife's death, and perhaps also because of his chronically painful back condition, he was far less animated in his public appearances. Yet since undergoing successful back surgery in 1995, his comedic timing and warm smile have returned to brighten his speeches. Some observers maintain that had his spouse survived, Rehnquist might have considered resigning from the Court to share retirement with her. Instead, now seventy-five, he shows no signs of leaving the high bench, especially while Democrat Bill Clinton remains in office. That occupant of the White

House provided Rehnquist with one of the sternest challenges of his long career—presiding over the Clinton impeachment trial in the Senate, as the Constitution requires the chief justice to do when the House impeaches the president. Rehnquist met this professional test with particular expertise, having published a book on impeachment (*Grand Inquests: The Historic Impeachments of Justice Samuel Chase and President Andrew Johnson*) in 1992. This, the second of his three books (the first, published in 1987, offered a brief history of the Supreme Court, and the third, appearing in 1998, examined the Court's jurisprudence during wartime) urges the Senate to recognize the constitutionally enshrined separation of powers in wielding its authority to remove presidents and federal judges.

Young Bill Rehnquist's elementary school declaration, "I'm going to change the government," was thus part wish, part prophecy. Now in his twenty-seventh year on the Court, he had been (up to 1999) probably the least well-known, most powerful official in the federal government. The chief justice, who has so assiduously opposed cameras in his courtroom, then suddenly found himself on television daily during Clinton's Senate trial. Though he attained new celebrity as a result of that historic event, Rehnquist's influential conservative jurisprudence had already guaranteed his place in the history books as an agent of change in American government and society.

ENDNOTES

1. George Lardner, Jr., and Saundra Saperstein, "Chief Justice-Designate Sought to Redirect U.S.," *Washington Post*, July 6, 1986, p. A12.
2. Ibid., p. A1.
3. Ibid., p. A12.
4. William H. Rehnquist, *The Supreme Court: How It Was, How It Is* (New York: Quill, 1987), p. 38.
5. William H. Rehnquist, "Who Writes Decisions of the Supreme Court?" *U.S. News & World Report,* December 13, 1957, p. 75.
6. George Lardner, Jr., "Rehnquist Got Call That Baker Missed for Nixon Court Nomination," *Washington Post*, December 18, 1998, p. A6.
7. Personal interview, Washington, D.C., September 24, 1985.
8. William H. Rehnquist, "Remarks on the Process of Judging," *Washington and Lee Law Review* 49 (Spring 1992): 264.
9. Ibid., 270.
10. 443 U.S. 193 (1979).
11. Qtd. in Craig M. Bradley, "William H. Rehnquist," in *The Supreme Court Justices' Illustrated Biographies, 1789–1995*, 2d ed., ed. Clare Cushman (Washington, D.C.: Congressional Quarterly, 1995), p. 499.
12. William H. Rehnquist, "'All Discord, Harmony Not Understood': The Performance of the Supreme Court of the United States," *Arizona Law Review* 22 (1980): 977.
13. See David J. Garrow's "The Rehnquist Years," *New York Times Magazine*, October 6, 1996, p. 66.
14. William H. Rehnquist, "Convocation Address, Wake Forest University," *Wake Forest Law Review* 29 (1994): 1005–06.
15. Qtd. in Barbara A. Perry and Henry J. Abraham, "The Reagan Supreme Court Appointees," in *Great Justices of the Supreme*

Court, ed. William Pederson and Norman Provizer (New York: Peter Lang, 1992), p. 331.

16. Al Kamen, "For Rehnquist, Aftermath of Confirmation Is Routine," *Washington Post*, September 19, 1986, p. A3.
17. Rehnquist, "'All Discord, Harmony Not Understood,'" 985.
18. Perry and Abraham, p. 332.
19. Tony Mauro, "Invoking the Wrath of Rehnquist," *Legal Times*, March 1995.
20. 491 U.S. 397 (1989).
21. Joan Biskupic, "Balance of Power," *Washington Post*, July 3, 1998, p. A17.

CHAPTER TWO

John Paul Stevens

A visitor to Justice John Paul Stevens's chambers at the U.S. Supreme Court is likely to find him dressed informally in a short-sleeved sport shirt, open at the collar. His mode of dress matches his demeanor—unpretentious, modest, welcoming. On the bench, he sports his trademark bow tie; and, with his silver-white hair combed straight back, the seventy-nine-year-old associate justice with the warm smile looks like everyone's favorite grandfather. As Stevens speaks in oral argument, his flat, Midwestern accent reveals his Illinois roots, and his respectful, yet keenly incisive, questions posed to attorneys appearing before the Court demonstrate the brilliant intellect that has marked his academic and professional pursuits.

Born April 20, 1920, in Chicago, Stevens was the youngest of Ernest James Stevens and Elizabeth Street Stevens's four sons. Elizabeth was an English teacher, and Ernest acquired his considerable wealth in the hotel and insurance businesses—at one time owning and managing the Stevens Hotel, which is now the stately Chicago Hilton on Michigan Avenue. The prominent Stevens family lived in the then-grand neighborhood surrounding the University of Chicago, and young John attended elementary and preparatory school at the university's Laboratory School. It obviously prepared him well, for he went on to graduate from the University of Chicago in 1941 *magna cum laude*, Phi Beta Kappa, and first in his class. At the university, he had majored in English, edited the student newspaper, and joined Psi Upsilon, the fraternity his father had pledged at Chicago. Fresh out of college, Stevens married his childhood sweetheart Elizabeth Jane Sheeran in 1942; their marriage lasted thirty-seven years and produced four children (John, Kathryn, Elizabeth, and Susan). The Stevens were divorced in 1979, and Justice Stevens married Maryan Mulholland Simon shortly thereafter.

Like most men of his generation, Stevens entered the military during World War II. From 1942 to 1945 he served in the United States Navy as a watch officer, analyzing and breaking the code of intercepted Japanese communications at Pearl Harbor *after* the infamous attack there. "For services in the Communications Intelligence Organization, the nature of which cannot be divulged," Stevens was awarded the Bronze Star.

Before the war, Stevens had considered following in his mother's footsteps by becoming a teacher, but one of his older brothers, an attorney, encouraged him to pursue a degree at Northwestern University Law School, which their father had attended. Duplicating his undergraduate success, John Stevens earned the highest grades in the law school's history, became editor of the law review, graduated first in his class and *magna cum laude*, and was elected to the Order of the Coif law honorary. After graduating from law school in 1947, Stevens continued on the most prestigious course in the law profession, serving a U.S. Supreme Court clerkship. From October 1947 to July 1948 he clerked for Justice Wiley Rutledge, a Franklin Roosevelt appointee and distinguished civil libertarian who, like Stevens, hailed from the Midwest. (Rutledge had been a personable and popular law professor and dean of the law schools at Washington University in St. Louis and the University of Iowa.)

Admitted to the Illinois bar in 1949, Stevens returned to his hometown to take a position at the leading Chicago law firm of Poppenhusen, Johnston, Thompson, and Raymond. He served as an associate there for three years, developing a well-regarded expertise in antitrust law. He also lectured on the subject at Northwestern and eventually at the University of Chicago law schools. In 1951 the future justice served as associate counsel for the U.S. House of Representatives' Subcommittee on the Study of Monopoly Power. He then became a named partner in his own firm of Rothschild, Stevens, Barry, and Myers, established in the early 1950s. While a partner there, Stevens also served as a member of the U.S. Attorney General's National Committee to Study the Antitrust Laws from 1953 to 1955. His reputation as a superb attorney of notable integrity spread, and in 1969 the Illinois Supreme Court appointed him chief counsel to a special commission investigating judicial impropriety among state judges.

The commission's work generated intense public scrutiny and brought Stevens's name to prominence. Based on the publicity, Senator Charles

Percy (R.–Ill.) called John Stevens to his office and told him that he would like to suggest his name for the U.S. Court of Appeals for the Seventh Circuit. Percy and Stevens were college friends who had lost touch, and the Illinois senator seemed unaware of their past association when he met with Stevens in 1969. Percy asked Stevens about his party affiliation, saying it would be easier if he were a Republican. Stevens replied that he came from a Republican family but had never run for office, so his partisan label was not public knowledge.[1] Earl Pollock, a prominent Chicago antitrust lawyer, once described Stevens as "almost a nonpolitical animal."[2] In 1970 President Richard Nixon nominated John Paul Stevens to his first judgeship, a position on the Seventh Circuit Court of Appeals.

Judge Stevens's tenure on the Court of Appeals produced approximately 200 opinions that were lengthy and filled with footnotes, reflecting his precise and detailed approach to the law. In substance, they were considered pragmatic, moderate, and imaginative. A body of Stevens's opinions that represented more conservative views caught the attention of President Gerald Ford's administration as they searched for a nominee to replace Justice William O. Douglas when ill health forced him to retire in 1975. On the circuit bench, for example, Stevens pragmatically argued in favor of a dress code for public-school teachers—not because he valued uniformity over individualism, but because he believed "that each choice between conformity and diversity is itself affected by a variety of factors, and local school boards need the freedom to make diverse choices for themselves."[3] Stevens has always been skeptical of broad judge-made formulas that limit the application of relevant facts in future cases.

The president's wife, Betty Ford, who became an outspoken advocate of women's causes during her husband's brief tenure as president after Nixon resigned in 1974, put public pressure on President Ford to name the first woman to the U.S. Supreme Court. The president consulted with Attorney General Edward H. Levi and White House Counsel Philip Buchen, requesting that they draft a list of potential nominees, and specifically instructing them to include female candidates. Ford then submitted an initial list to the American Bar Association's Committee on Judiciary for a preliminary review. They declared the list "a good one, which was responsibly drawn." It contained the names of two members of Congress and five federal circuit court judges, including Stevens, but no female candidates. The administration submitted a second list of possible nominees, including two women circuit judges. The final choice narrowed to two candidates: Judge Stevens and Judge Arlin M. Adams of the Third Circuit Court of Appeals, who had appeared on the initial list; Ford chose the former after a final consultation with Levi and Buchen. (Levi had asked Stevens to lecture at the University of Chicago when Levi was dean of the law school there.)

Stevens recalls that he had met President Ford for the first time only a few days before the nomination. The occasion was a White House dinner for the federal judiciary, where Stevens chatted with Ford over drinks and during the post-dinner dance when Ford circulated to Stevens's table. They discussed the New York City debt crisis and whether the federal government should bail out the Big Apple. Although Ford exhibited no special interest in Stevens that night, the president called him at the end of the week with the stunning news of his nomination. Typically modest in his assessment of the factors leading to his appointment, Stevens simply avows that he was a "noncontroversial, Midwestern, appellate court judge."[4] The lack of controversy that marked Stevens and his career was indeed determinative. Chief Justice Warren Burger wanted to expedite the process of filling the seat vacated by Douglas in the middle of the 1975–76 term after months of absence due to his long illness. Moreover, the White House desired a smooth confirmation to place Ford's nominee on the Supreme Court *before* the 1976 presidential election in case Ford lost (which, of course, he did; the winner, Jimmy Carter, had no opportunities to nominate a justice to the high bench during his four-year term).

In announcing Stevens's nomination to the public on November 28, 1975, Ford called the circuit court judge "the best qualified [candidate]. . . . Judge Stevens is held in the highest esteem by his colleagues in the legal profession and the judiciary and has had an outstanding career in the practice and teaching of law as well as on the federal bench."[5] After a thorough analysis of his circuit court opinions, the ABA's committee rated Stevens "highly qualified" by virtue of his "high standards of professional competence, judicial temperament and integrity." Awarding their highest evaluation to Stevens, the ABA panel announced that Stevens's lower-court opinions "show a uniformly high degree of scholarship, discipline, and conscientiousness."[6]

During the three days of hearings before the Senate Judiciary Committee, Judge Stevens asserted that he would follow the same policy of "judicial restraint" on the Supreme Court that he had adhered to on the court of appeals, where his opinions demonstrated respect for established procedures rather than for any particular ideology. He commented, "It's always been my philosophy to decide cases on the narrowest grounds possible and not to reach out."[7] Describing the role of a judge, Stevens argued before the Judiciary Committee that jurists did not "have a charter" to substitute their own views for the law. Judges should confine themselves to "deciding no more than the specific controversy" presented by the case before them. He predicted that he would be "most reluctant to depart from prior precedent without a clear showing" that a departure was necessary. Although Stevens noted that he placed a "very high value on the First Amendment," he admitted that "there are occasions when restrictions [on the press] are justified by national security," such as in the reporting of troop movements.[8] At a time when the states were debating the Equal Rights Amendment, Stevens maintained that amending the Constitution should be eschewed when legislation could achieve the same goals sought by the constitutional change. Predictably, women's groups advocating passage of the ERA criticized Stevens's nomination. Nevertheless, the Judiciary Committee approved him by a vote of 13–0, and sent his name to the full Senate, which confirmed him within a week by the unanimous vote of 98–0.

Stevens's confirmation, coming just sixteen days after President Ford officially submitted his name to the Senate for its constitutionally mandated role to "advise and consent," was one of the fastest for any of the justices then sitting on the Supreme Court. It would be among the last in the final quarter of the twentieth century to sail so smoothly through the nomination and appointment process. On December 19, 1975, John Paul Stevens, at age fifty-five, took the oath of office to assume the ninth seat on the Supreme Court. As his colleagues aged and postponed retirement, Stevens remained in the most junior position on the bench for six years.

(Justice Sandra Day O'Connor would finally break the nomination hiatus with her landmark appointment in 1981.)

Upon Stevens's nomination to the Supreme Court, the press correctly noted that he was neither a partisan nor an ideologue. His record on the high court over his twenty-four-year tenure (second in seniority only to Chief Justice Rehnquist) has defied simplistic classification. In terms of opinion production, his first four months on the Court were illustrative; he was the most prolific opinion-writer among his colleagues. Whereas freshmen justices typically maintain a low profile, Stevens wrote nine opinions, including four dissents from conservative majority opinions in the first half of his initial term on the high tribunal. Indeed, Stevens's early voting pattern pleasantly surprised civil libertarians. Women's rights groups that had feared that Stevens was insensitive to gender discrimination commended him after his first two terms on the Court for his votes and opinions favoring civil rights for women. In the term ending in June 1977, Stevens sided with the Court's staunchest liberals (Justices William Brennan and Thurgood Marshall) nearly 60 percent of the time.

In women's rights cases, Justice Stevens has typically voted on the side upholding the cause of gender equity. The 1976 *General Electric Co. v. Gilbert* case found him in dissent (along with Brennan and Marshall) from the Court's opinion that a private employer's disability plan excluding pregnancy from coverage is not invidiously discriminatory. The three dissenters were vindicated when Congress overturned the Court's ruling with legislation. In another 1976 decision, *Craig v. Boren*, Stevens was with the majority in voting to strike down an Oklahoma law that banned the sale of "3.2 beer" to men under twenty-one but allowed sales to women over eighteen. Stevens joined Justices Brennan, Marshall, and White in dissenting from the Court's Rehnquist-led majority, which upheld California's statutory-rape law punishing males, but not females, for sexual intercourse with an underage partner of the opposite sex. The Supreme Court in *Michael M. v. Superior Court* deemed the disparate treatment of men and women not irrational because "only women may become pregnant."

Justice Stevens maintained a pro-choice position in the contentious abortion litigation that has come before the Court. He dissented from the Court's energized conservative faction in 1989 when it upheld Missouri's attempts to limit abortions in *Webster v. Reproductive Health Services*, and he would have gone a step further than the controlling plurality in 1992's *Planned Parenthood of Southeastern Pennsylvania v. Casey* to reaffirm the trimester system of *Roe v. Wade*, which had allowed virtually unlimited access to abortions in the first three months of pregnancy.

Civil rights issues involving race are more typical of Stevens's case-by-case analysis of constitutional and statutory interpretation. He disappointed affirmative-action proponents by his vote in the landmark *Bakke* case to invalidate the University of California at Davis Medical School's quota system for admitting minorities. (Justice Lewis Powell's controlling opinion struck down the use of quotas but upheld the balance of the affirmative-action program, with race to be used as a "plus" factor in admissions.) Stevens abstained from voting in the 1979 *Weber* case, in which Justice Brennan upheld a private employer's affirmative-action plan over the challenge from a white worker who had been exluded from an apprentice-training program solely based on race. The next year Stevens dissented in *Fullilove v. Klutznick* from the majority's ruling in favor of Congress's 10-percent set-aside quota for "minority business enterprises" in federal construction contracts. Stevens's angry dissent, which he read from the bench the day the decision came down, labelled the set-aside law "perverse" and compared it to the Nazi laws that defined who was a Jew.

Justice Stevens continued to vote against minority racial preferences until 1986–87, when he joined the Court's liberal faction (consisting of Justices Brennan, Marshall, Blackmun, and sometimes Powell) to support affirmative-action programs then under attack by the Reagan administration. In 1989 Stevens reverted to his *Fullilove* position, however, in joining the conservative justices in *Croson* to strike down a *local* set-aside quota that required 30 percent of Richmond, Virginia construction contracts to be let to minority-owned companies. The very next year, Stevens switched sides again, this time in *Metro Broadcasting v. Federal Communications Commission*. Following Justice Brennan's leadership in his last opinion before retirement, Stevens voted to *uphold* the F.C.C.'s affirmative-action policy to increase minority ownership of broadcast licenses. Revealing his fact-based approach to cases, Stevens argued in his brief concurring opinion that *Fullilove* differed from *Metro Broadcasting* because the latter concerned an area (broadcasting) where racial and ethnic characteristics are truly relevant.

How would the mercurial Stevens vote in 1995's *Adarand Constructors v. Peña*, which again challenged federal set-aside programs? If he held to his positions in *Fullilove* and *Croson*, he would vote to invalidate the program. Yet he was more recently on record as supporting the minority-preference scheme in *Metro Broadcasting*. Although Justices Antonin Scalia and Clarence Thomas wanted to strike down *all* such racial classifications, Justice Sandra Day O'Connor's opinion for the Court in *Adarand* argued that such classifications could survive "strict scrutiny" (the highest level of judicial examination under the Fourteenth Amendment's Equal Protection Clause) *if* the government could prove a compelling state interest in classifying on the basis of race. O'Connor declared that a general policy of "racial diversity" could not meet the "compelling" test. Her decision also explicitly overruled the *Metro Broadcasting* precedent and declared *Fullilove* to be no longer controlling. Justice Stevens (the senior associate justice among the dissenters, which included Justices Souter, Ginsburg, and Breyer) wrote the lead dissent, urging adherence to precedent, including *Fullilove*; distinction between *federal* set-aside programs (justifiable) and *state* set-aside mandates (unjustifiable); and recognition of "invidious" discrimination in the workplace, in contrast to efforts at merely promoting "diversity."

Civil rights advocates have also had reason to cheer Stevens in the 1990's cases challenging so-called majority-minority voting districts. While the more conservative bloc on the high court has taken a skeptical view toward bizarrely shaped districts drawn with race as the predominant criterion, Stevens has joined the liberal bloc in dissent, arguing that race-based districts are necessary to ensure fair representation of minorities in Congress and state legislatures.

In First Amendment free-expression and free press-cases, Stevens has applied his patented nondoctrinaire analysis. Among his first decisions for the Court in this realm was his majority opinion in *Federal Communications Commission v. Pacifica Foundation*. The 1978 case arose out of litigation over a complaint lodged with the FCC by a father who, while driving with his young son, inadvertently tuned his car radio to a monologue by comedian George Carlin on the "seven dirty words" that cannot be used on television. To the father's shock and embarrassment, Carlin articulated each word in the septet, none of which a parent would want his young child to hear or repeat. The FCC agreed with the complaint and prohibited radio transmission of such "offensive—indecent but not obscene—words" during so-called "family hours." Stevens, writing the majority opinion for himself, Chief Justice Burger and Justices Powell, Blackmun, and Rehnquist, upheld the FCC's decision. He noted that words "patently, offensively, referring to excretory and sexual organs and activities" could be banned from radio broadcasts, which intrude upon "the privacy of the home [or car], where the individual's right to be left alone plainly outweighs the First Amendment rights of an intruder."[9] The words at issue were not in a book or theater production that an adult had voluntarily chosen to view.

The distinction between willful and inadvertent exposure to material was dispositive for Stevens in writing the majority's 1997 opinion striking down the Communications Decency Act, which marked Congress's attempt to protect minors from "indecent" and "patently offensive" communications on the Internet. Though the oldest member of the Court in the late 1990s, Stevens was among the first justices to embrace word processing, and he drafts his opinions at his computer keyboard. Clearly, he understood Internet technology in declaring that the "'odds are slim'" that a user would enter a sexually explicit site by accident. He thus distinguished Websites from radio or television broadcasts, which could bombard an unsuspecting listener or viewer. In contrast, "'the Internet requires a series of affirmative steps more deliberate and directed than merely turning a dial.'" Stevens concluded for the Court in *Reno v. American Civil Liberties Union* that "[n]otwithstanding the legitimacy and importance of the congressional goal of protecting children from harmful materials . . . the statute abridges 'the freedom of speech' protected by the First Amendment."[10]

On the issue of flag-burning as a form of political protest, however, Stevens voted twice (in 1989's *Texas v. Johnson* and 1990's *U.S. v. Eichman*) to uphold flag-protection legislation at both the state and federal levels. Each time, he dissented with Chief Justice Rehnquist and Justices White and O'Connor, arguing that burning an American flag as a

)

symbolic protest was *not* a form of expression protected by the First Amendment's free *speech* guarantee.

Nevertheless, beyond flag-burning, Stevens has been a visible advocate for free expression rights. He dissented from the Court's decision upholding a ban against abortion advice by federally funded family planning clinics in *Rust v. Sullivan*; wrote the opinion for a unanimous decision in *City of Ladue v. Gilleo*, invalidating a local ordinance banning all yard signs except ten specified types (including realtors' signs); voted with the rest of the Court in *Rubin v. Coors Brewing Co.* to strike down the Federal Alcohol Administration Act's prohibition against advertising alcohol content on beer; and wrote for the Court's unanimous invalidation of Rhode Island's ban on advertising liquor prices in *44 Liquormart v. Rhode Island.*

Under the First Amendment's Establishment Clause, Stevens has supported a high wall between church and state, as demonstrated by his *Wallace v. Jaffree* opinion for the Supreme Court in 1985, striking down Alabama's statute authorizing a one-minute period of silence in all public schools "for meditation or prayer," and his vote with Justices Kennedy, Blackmun, O'Connor, and Souter declaring nonsectarian prayers at public-school graduations in violation of Amendment I. Stevens has been less reliable in upholding individual or group free-exercise-of-religion claims. He voted with the majority in the notable *Oregon v. Smith* case to uphold the state's controlled-substances ban that "indicentally" interferred with Native Americans' liturgical use of peyote, a hallucinogenic drug. He sided with the majority striking down the Religious Freedom Restoration Act in 1997's *City of Boerne v. Flores*. RFRA had been Congress's effort to overturn the *Smith* decision by resurrecting the "compelling state interest" test to void laws that infringe, even incidentally, on religious exercises. When the city of Hialeah, Florida banned animal sacrifices, however, Justice Stevens followed his unanimous colleagues in *Church of the Lukumi Babalu Aye v. Hialeah*, the 1993 ruling that declared the ordinance unconstitutional because it was clearly aimed at the Cuban-American sect that sacrificed animals as part of their liturgy.

Although Stevens's persistent junior status during his first six years on the Court and his frequently idiosyncratic perception of the law combined to dilute his impact on American jurisprudence, he has written several resonant opinions in the 1990s that reflect his increased seniority and occasional leadership of the newly emergent liberal bloc, consisting of Justices Souter, Ginsburg, and Breyer. Stevens authored the Court's ruling in *Bavarian Motor Works v. Gore,* which declared that a car owner's $2 million award against BMW for a flawed paint job was "grossly excessive" and violated the Constitution. He also wrote the astonishingly unanimous decision in the *Clinton v. Jones* case, asserting that the president was *not* entitled to immunity in the Paula Jones sexual-harassment suit during his White House tenure. Justice Stevens made headlines in 1995 with his ruling for the narrowly divided Court striking down *state* term limits for members of Congress in *U.S. Term Limits, Inc. v. Thornton.* He argued that such limits, which nearly half of the states had adopted, violated the constitutionally mandated uniformity of the federal system. He thus sided with the dissenters in 1997 against the majority's view in *Printz v. U.S.* that struck down several of the federally required gun-control provisions of the Brady Act.

Still, Stevens's opinion statistics portray his independent role on the Supreme Court through the 1997–98 term. Although he has produced 313 opinions for the majority, he has drafted 301 concurring and 511 dissenting opinions. The last figure represents more dissents than seven of his colleagues put together. Chief Justice Rehnquist has authored 286 dissents in his twenty-seven years on the Court—far behind Stevens, who has been on the high bench three fewer years than the chief.[11]

Long after most individuals his age have entered retirement, Stevens gives no indication of leaving the Court (as of early 1999). He maintains a home in Florida and spends most of his time there when the Court is not in session. He continues to be an active participant in oral arguments, aways maintaining his self-effacing, considerate attitude toward counsel appearing before the imposing high tribunal. Yet his respectful demeanor belies his unique perspective on cases. As Stevens explains his role in the public work of the Court: "You have a point in mind that you think may not have been brought out . . . but you want to be sure your colleagues don't overlook that so . . . you'll ask a question to bring it out, and you're not necessarily trying to sell everybody on the position, but you want everybody to have at least the point in mind."[12] Though John Paul Stevens has the intellect and charm to be a Brennan-like coalition builder on the Supreme Court, he has relished the part of the judicial maverick, willing to roam freely over the legal landscape and refusing to be fenced in by any ideological or jurisprudential blocs.

ENDNOTES

1. Personal interview, Washington, D.C., September 12, 1985.
2. Qtd. in Stephen Isaacs, "Specialist in Antitrust Law," *Washington Post*, November 29, 1975.
3. *Miller v. School District*, 495 F.2d 658 (1974), qtd. in Robert Judd Sickels, *John Paul Stevens and the Constitution: The Search for Balance* (University Park, Pa.: Pennsylvania State University Press, 1988), p. 7.
4. Personal interview, Washington, D.C., September 12, 1985.
5. "Stevens Picked for Court Vacancy," (Charlottesville, Va.) *Daily Progress*, November 29, 1975, p. A1.
6. See Spencer Rich, "Ford Picks Chicago Jurist," *Washington Post*, November 29, 1975, pp. A1, A4.
7. Qtd. in Lesley Oelsner, "Justice Stevens Questions Equal Rights Amendment," *New York Times*, December 9, 1975, p. 1.
8. Qtd. in Lesley Oelsner, "Stevens Calls Court Pay Too Low; Puts His Net Worth at $171,284," *New York Times*, December 10, 1975, p. 5.
9. 438 U.S. 726.
10. 117 S.Ct. 2329.
11. Henry J. Abraham, *Justices, Presidents, and Senators: A History of Appointments to the Supreme Court*, 4th ed. (Lanham, Md.: Rowman & Littlefield, 1999).
12. Qtd. in York Associates Television, Inc. (producer), *The Supreme Court of the United States* (Washington, D.C.: Supreme Court Historical Society, 1997), video.

CHAPTER THREE

Sandra Day O'Connor

Because of her status as the first female member of the Supreme Court of the United States, Justice Sandra Day O'Connor has become an international icon. She is much in demand as a speaker and has delivered addresses in all fifty states and many foreign countries. After speaking to a large group gathered on a snowy day in North Dakota, she was approached by parents who wanted her to touch their children. These requests for a laying on of hands speak volumes about the reverence Americans maintain toward her. Respect for Justice O'Connor knows no borders. The justices of the Supreme Court of India visited their U.S. counterparts in 1995. The male Indian justices sedately toured the American Supreme Court building while their sari-clad wives deferentially walked several paces behind. When Justice O'Connor welcomed the group at a small reception, however, the wives eagerly crowded around her, telling her what a hero she was to them.

Even without her pathbreaking appointment to the Supreme Court in 1981, the story of Justice O'Connor's life would make fascinating reading, especially if it focused on her childhood. For two generations before Sandra's birth, the Day family had raised cattle on the Lazy B Ranch, almost 200,000 acres of desert Southwest countryside on the border of Arizona and New Mexico. The nearest town to the small, rustic adobe house on the property was Duncan, a wide spot in the road twenty-five miles away. Her father, Harry A. Day, who left Stanford University when his father died suddenly, took on the job of managing the ranch. Conservative by nature, he was committed to fighting the elements and the federal government regulations that plagued his land. He married Ada Mae Wilkey, the daughter of a general-store owner in Duncan, when she finished her education at the University of Arizona. Both Harry and Ada Mae had inquisitive minds; they read widely and engaged in lively discussions.

On March 26, 1930, their daughter Sandra was born in El Paso, Texas, where her mother had gone for the event so as not to give birth on the isolated ranch. Sandra loved growing up at the Lazy B, exploring the intriguing countryside on horseback, herding cattle, and interacting with the colorful farm hands who lived on the ranch. Her two siblings, a brother and a sister, were not born until the late 1930s, so she was the focus of her parents' affection for the first eight years of her childhood. Her adventurous preschool days ended, however, when her parents took her to live with her Grandmother Wilkey in El Paso so Sandra could attend the exclusive Radford School for Girls. She was an excellent student but longed for the summers when she was allowed to return to her beloved parents and life on the ranch. She attended high school closer to home in Lordsburg, New Mexico, but with her precocious mind she accelerated her program in the public school there and finished in just two years.

Fulfilling her father's own dream of a Stanford education, she enrolled in the California university at age sixteen. Her major was economics, but she was most intrigued by a business law course taught by Professor Stanley Rathbun, who preached that pursuing individual destiny through community service and familial devotion could create a better world. Having been raised in an environment where one's life was at the mercy of harsh elements, young Sandra was mesmerized by Rathbun's gospel of self-actualization. To this day, she speaks movingly about the impact that inspiring teachers can have on their students.

Rathbun encouraged Sandra Day to pursue a law degree at Stanford Law School. After receiving her undergraduate degree *magna cum laude* in 1950 at age twenty, she took Rathbun's advice. In a law school class of about 150, she was one of only five women—all grudgingly given spaces that the faculty thought should go to men. Indeed, a photo of some of her classmates from that era pictures her in a 1950s-style shirtwaist dress with only one other female student. Also in the picture is her future colleague on the Supreme Court, William H. Rehnquist. A bright and popular student, Sandra Day made law review along with Rehnquist and even dated him for a while. They stopped dating after a visit to the ranch, when her parents reportedly discouraged the relationship because they said the future chief justice had poor table manners!

A new relationship developed, however, with John Jay O'Connor III, a fellow student and member of the law review. The couples' eyes still light up when they recall their meeting and subsequent courtship. A usually tedious assignment for the law review, checking citations for articles, provided their first chance to become acquainted. Mr. O'Connor remembers that Sandra was attractive and laughed at his jokes, so he asked her out for a beer at the end of the evening. That first date led to their seeing each other for the next forty evenings. Only when John's work began to suffer did the couple take some time away from their new romance. Sandra continued to do well in her classes and graduated in 1952 with election to the Order of the Coif, *the* honorary society for outstanding law students.

Despite her exemplary academic record, Day collided with the gender discrimination extant in the legal profession in the 1950s and was unsuccessful in finding a law firm that would hire a female associate. In fact, her only job offer from the private-practice realm was for a legal secretary's position. Justice O'Connor expresses no bitterness about the roadblocks she encountered in her early career. Yet she admits to having come to a firsthand "realization that opportunities [for women] were limited."[1] Although she was surprised at the professional discrimination that she faced, having encountered no overt sexism at Stanford, she simply turned to the public sector to pursue her career. In hindsight, she now recognizes the increased opportunities she had as a public servant that she might well have missed in a private law firm. Moreover, she was able to implement Professor Rathbun's formula for a fulfilling life. Thus, her first job was as deputy county attorney in San Mateo County, California, from 1952 to 1953. In 1996 the county's historical society asked her for permission to display her job application letter. The justice reported how embarrassed she was when she read the letter forty-four years after she first authored it. She admitted, "I was simply amazed. If I received that letter from a young law clerk, I'd have thrown it out. I'd say she is obviously a nut. I poured out my whole life story. I really wanted that job."[2]

Day got it and plunged into her new career while planning her marriage to John O'Connor, who graduated one year after her from Stanford Law School. The wedding took place in a simple ceremony at the

Lazy B in December 1952. The couple moved to Germany the next year when John was drafted into the Army. While he served in the Judge Advocate General Corps, Sandra worked as a civilian lawyer for the Quartermaster in Frankfurt for three years. When they returned to the United States, they decided to settle in Phoenix, at that time a moderate-sized state capital where they thought they could raise a family and contribute to a community that was on the verge of a civic and population boom. Their first son, Scott, was born in 1958, and they had two more sons, Brian and Jay, in 1960 and 1962. While John progressed through the ranks at a prominent Phoenix law firm, Sandra was still unable to get a position in the private sector, so she started a two-person law office with a young attorney she met while taking the Arizona bar exam.

After her first two sons were born, however, she found it increasingly difficult to find reliable baby-sitters, so she decided to take time off from her full-time professional work and look after her children. During her five-year break from the job market, she was alert to the problems of losing touch with her profession; she kept her skills and contacts up to date by accepting occasional legal and philanthropic work. Among other tasks, she wrote and graded bar exam questions, chaired a local bar association lawyer-referral service, volunteered for the Republican Party (and befriended Barry Goldwater in the process), served on her county's planning and zoning commission, and became active in the Junior League.

In 1965 Sandra O'Connor was ready to reenter the world of full-time legal practice, and she did so with a position as an assistant attorney general for the state of Arizona. Although she was given the most difficult job in the office, sorting out the legal problems of the Arizona state mental hospital, she handled the job with her usual expertise and aplomb. In addition, she continued her volunteer work and was elected president of the Junior League's Phoenix chapter in 1967. Her numerous professional and extracurricular activities, combined with supervising her three young boys, resulted in her cutting her job to three-quarters hours so she could leave the office in mid-afternoon. Throughout these years John O'Connor was a supportive husband, proudly touting his wife's achievements while becoming a highly successful attorney himself. Although the bolstering of his wife's career was atypical for many men of his generation, he did leave most of the traditional household chores to Sandra. She is a superb cook and organized her grocery shopping and dinner preparation with such precision that her sons remember sitting down to delicious meals with their parents virtually every night of the week.

But their mother's career path took an even busier turn when she was named to the Arizona Senate in 1969 to fill an unexpired term. She then won two elections to her seat and eventually became Senate Republican majority leader—the first woman in the nation to hold such a position. She was true to her father's conservative roots and her own Republican Party credentials, but the lessons of Professor Rathbun had been learned well, and she could be progressive when she thought the community would benefit from reform. She was a sure supporter of women's rights, calling for Arizona's ratification of the Equal Rights Amendment. Her perseverance, sheer hard work, attention to detail, and conciliatory approach to the legislative process made her a successful state senator, although sometimes she was more judicious than the average politician. Still, her political instincts seemed sharp, and there was even talk that she might run for the governorship. Deciding that such a position would work too much of a hardship on her and her family, she opted for a judicial career, winning election to the Maricopa County Superior Court in Phoenix in 1975. Four years later Democratic Governor Bruce Babbitt nominated her to the Arizona Court of Appeals, one step below the state's Supreme Court. As a judge, O'Connor displayed the same characteristics that had governed her entire life: she was scrupulously fair, tough in meting out justice, and supremely efficient.

In the late 1970s the O'Connors' broad social and professional circle, which they had cultivated since arriving in Phoenix, made a serendipitous connection. Friends of the O'Connors invited them to spend the weekend on Lake Powell with Chief Justice Warren Burger, who was making a trip to Arizona. "The Chief" (as Burger liked to be called) and Sandra hit it off immediately, and he later claimed, "[I]t was on Lake Powell that I sized Sandra up and decided that she should have the next appointment to the Court."[3] Thus far, the historical record does not indicate that Burger had a role to play in O'Connor's ultimate appointment, but when Justice Potter Stewart publicly announced his retirement from the Supreme Court in June 1981, the Arizona judge was already on the list of potential nominees. Facing the so-called gender gap in the 1980 presidential campaign, Ronald Reagan, despite his repudiation of Jimmy Carter's policy of gender and race representation in the federal judiciary, promised to fill one of the first Supreme Court vacancies in his administration with a qualified woman. His advisers had begun to collect names of suitable women nominees as soon as Stewart alerted them to his pending retirement in April 1981.

Reagan's attorney general, William French Smith, whose law firm had offered O'Connor the legal secretary's position upon law school graduation, sent his chief counselor, Kenneth Starr, and a special assistant to Phoenix to interview Judge O'Connor as well as Arizonans who were familiar with her personal and professional background. The attorney general received a highly favorable report regarding her credentials and ideological compatibility, and he phoned O'Connor to invite her to Washington. She was in bed recovering from surgery for a hysterectomy but received approval from her physician to make the trip to Washington. On July 1 Judge O'Connor and President Reagan met in the Oval Office, and she quickly reminded him that they had first met a decade earlier when he was governor of California and she was in the Arizona Senate. They reportedly had a productive hour-long chat at the White House, and on July 7 Reagan made his historic announcement nominating the fifty-one-year-old Arizona jurist to the Supreme Court. The president pronounced O'Connor "truly a 'person for all seasons,' possessing those unique qualities of temperament, fairness, intellectual capacity and devotion to the public good which have characterized the 101 'brethren' who have preceded her."[4]

Women's rights groups and prominent liberals, such as Senator Edward M. Kennedy (D.–Mass.) and Congressman Morris K. Udall (D.–Ariz.), were quick to announce their support for the first woman to be nominated to the highest court in the land. Udall praised her moderation, noting that it was the most that could be expected from the conservative Reagan administration. The traditional wing of the Republican Party, led by Senator Barry Goldwater (R.–Ariz.), professed its support for O'Connor, but the Christian Right sector of the party protested several of O'Connor's proabortion votes during her tenure in the state legislature. The Reverend Jerry Falwell called on "good Christians" to oppose O'Connor. Senator Goldwater's response was characteristically blunt: "Every good Christian ought to kick Falwell right in the ass."[5]

During her Senate confirmation hearings, O'Connor called her vote in the Arizona legislature to decriminalize abortion a mistake. She refused, however, to say how she would vote on the issue if it were to come before the Court. She did express her personal views in support of the death penalty and her opposition to busing to achieve racial integration. O'Connor also stated her belief in a restrained role for the federal judiciary: "I do not believe it is the function of the judiciary to step in and change the law because the times have changed. I do well understand the difference between legislating and judging. As a judge, it is not my function to develop public policy."[6] Just prior to her nomination, O'Connor had expressed in the *William and Mary Law Review* her approbation of Supreme Court decisions that required federal judges to defer to findings of fact by state courts.

Despite the ABA's qualified endorsement of her nomination (she was thought to have limited experience as a judge and practicing attorney), the Senate Judiciary Committee voted 17–0 to approve her appointment. On September 22, 1981, the full Senate voted 99–0 to confirm Sandra Day O'Connor as the first woman justice of the Supreme Court of the United States. Three days later she took the oath of office and smiled proudly as Chief Justice Warren Burger took her by the arm and led her down the steps of the Supreme Court building to meet the waiting media. Several years later, O'Connor modestly described her unprecedented nomination as having been a case of being "the right person in the right spot at the right time. Stated simply, you must be lucky."[7] But from her unique childhood on the Lazy B to her superb education to her persistence in combining homemaking and a public-service career, Sandra Day O'Connor had manufactured much of her luck and destiny.

Although Justice O'Connor remembers that she was treated cordially and with kindness by her new colleagues at the Supreme Court, the transition to the highest tribunal in the land was not easy. As she has stated, "There is no 'How to do it manual' for the Supreme Court," so she and her first clerk, Ruth McGregor, who had worked with John O'Connor for many years, had to muddle through. "We did not know how opinions were circulated; we did not know how the cert.[iorari] pool worked; we didn't know how anything worked," recalls the first woman justice.[8] Her colleague, Justice Lewis Powell, came to the rescue by offering her one of his secretaries to help with the paperwork. Powell thus earned O'Connor's eternal gratitude; when they danced at a function celebrating her appointment, the *Washington Post* impishly reported that the occasion was the first time two Supreme Court justices danced together.

Despite her unease in negotiating the mores of the Supreme Court, O'Connor characteristically worked tirelessly to master her new position. Although she would initially read most of her questions from the bench, she struck observers as having done her homework for each oral argument. She also pursued her physical well-being by starting and regularly participating in an aerobics class for female employees at the Court. Now approaching her seventieth birthday, she continues to participate each morning that her schedule allows, and she prods others to join her.

Justice O'Connor has generally lived up to President Reagan's expectations when he appointed her as a moderate conservative. In her first term on the Court (1981–82), she voted 77 percent of the time with the conservative bloc. Like most freshman justices, she contributed the smallest number of majority opinions in that first term, but she authored the fourth-highest number of concurring opinions.[9] The latter statistic signaled her tendency to see issues in a different light from the majority, a trend that has marked her entire service on the Court. In 1997–98 she was a member of the conservative alignment, consisting of Chief Justice Rehnquist and Justices Kennedy, Scalia, and Thomas, that made up the majority in most of the fifteen cases that were decided by 5–4 votes. In non-unanimous cases, she voted with Rehnquist and Kennedy 64 percent of the time.[10]

O'Connor's narrow vision of the federal judiciary's role is exemplified by her reliance on standing, the doctrine that requires a personal, concrete injury to the party who brings a suit to court. While the doctrine is a part of the classic formulation of judicial self-restraint, determining the existence of standing can be a highly subjective matter. In *Allen v. Wright*, a 1984 case in which parents of black public school children brought a nationwide class-action suit challenging the Internal

Revenue Service's allegedly inadequate measures to deny tax-exempt status to racially discriminatory private schools, O'Connor's opinion for the Court ruled that the parents did not have standing. She explained that the parents had not proved a direct harm to themselves or their children; moreover, the executive branch was responsible for carrying out the laws (in this case, IRS regulations), not the judiciary.

On matters of federalism, Justice O'Connor clung to her vision of a balance of power between the federal and state governments by dissenting vigorously in 1985's *Garcia v. San Antonio Metropolitan Transit Authority*, which held that the federal Fair Labor Standards Act's minimum wage and overtime provisions were applicable to San Antonio's transit authority. The former state legislator argued that "state legislative and administrative bodies are not field offices of the national bureaucracy," and she asserted that the federal and state governments must maintain their "separate and independent existence."[11] O'Connor voted with the majority in striking down the Gun-Free School Zones Act as an unconstitutional exercise of Congress's interstate commerce power in *U.S. v. Lopez*, a landmark 1995 case. Not surprisingly, she joined the dissent from the Court's other watershed federalism case in 1995, *U.S. Term Limits, Inc. v. Thornton*, which struck down laws in twenty-two states setting term limits for their federal officeholders in Congress. And guided by her reasoning in *Garcia*, she concurred in the Court's 1997 decision to strike down the Brady Handgun Act's unfunded mandate on state and local authorities to keep administrative records of handgun sales.

The issue of gender, however, tends to pull Justice O'Connor off the conservative reservation. She finds an active role for the federal judiciary and departs from validation of state policy and power when gender equality is at stake. During her first term, she cast the deciding vote in *Arizona v. Norris* that henceforth required equal treatment of men and women in monthly annuity-benefit payments under insurance pension plans, such as those in her home state of Arizona. Her first majority opinion in a gender discrimination case also came in her initial term on the Court. Interestingly, the case was brought by a man, Joe Hogan, against the all-female admissions policy of a state university in Mississippi. In the groundbreaking *Mississippi University for Women v. Hogan* decision, she wrote for a 5–4 majority that MUW's policy violated Mr.

Hogan's right to equal protection of the laws under the Fourteenth Amendment. She was also in the majority when her new female colleague, Ruth Bader Ginsburg, authored the 1996 decision striking down Virginia Military Institute's all-male admissions policy. In sexual harassment cases, she found for the Court in 1993 that creation of a hostile work environment may constitute actionable harassment under the Civil Rights Act's antidiscrimination section, but in 1997 she drafted the Court's opinion in a case that limited school districts' liability under a different law (Title IX) in sexual harassment suits involving their teachers. When asked if her own history of facing gender discrimination has shaped her opinions in these cases, Justice O'Connor cites the truism that "each of us is the sum total and product of our experiences." But she stresses that she cannot respond that her experiences affected her views in individual cases, which she attempts to decide from an "objective legal viewpoint."[12]

In the related realm of abortion policy, Justice O'Connor's previous experience as a legislator is most in evidence. In Solomonic fashion, she attempts to split the difference and find the middle ground that will allow a compromise to be forged.[13] In the 1983 case of *Akron v. Akron Center for Reproductive Health, Inc.*, the Court declared various local regulations on the performance of abortions to be unconstitutional as a violation of a women's right to privacy and the resultant right to decide whether to terminate her pregnancy as established in *Roe v. Wade*. Joined in a vigorous dissent by Justices Rehnquist and Byron White (the two dissenters in *Roe*), O'Connor attacked the majority opinion's steadfast maintenance of *Roe*'s trimester system whereby women's rights to abortion depended on which three-month sector of pregnancy they were in when they sought the procedure. She argued that no constitutional theory could support the trimester system; moreover, it cast judges in the roles of doctors attempting to sort out the biological and technological aspects of medical treatment of pregnancy and abortion. O'Connor conceded that women do have a right to privacy but that it only protects them from "unduly burdensome" limitations on access to abortion.

When Justice Antonin Scalia, a staunch antiabortion nominee, joined the Supreme Court in 1986, he hoped to count O'Connor as a sure vote to overturn the *Roe v. Wade* precedent. The opportunity to do so presented itself in the 1989 case of *Webster v. Reproductive Health Services*.

Justice O'Connor provided the crucial fifth vote to uphold Missouri's restrictions on access to abortion services because, in her view, they did not unduly burden women seeking the procedure. Her concurring opinion, however, refused to undertake a reexamination of *Roe*. For her cautious approach to one of the Court's most controversial precedents she was castigated by Justice Scalia's concurrence, which harshly characterized her thinking as "irresponsible," "irrational," and "not to be taken seriously."[14]

Inevitably, back to the Court came additional state limitations and regulations on access to abortion in *Planned Parenthood of Southeastern Pennsylvania v. Casey*. In a highly unusual step, Justices O'Connor, Souter, and Kennedy drafted, and then read from the bench, their controlling plurality opinion in the 1992 case. It upheld most of the Pennsylvania restrictions, but asserted that the central holding of *Roe* must remain intact in order to follow the Court's tradition of confirming its own precedents as a way of protecting its legitimacy. Moreover, the trio's opinion noted the practical fact of life that society had come to rely on the right established in *Roe*. O'Connor did contribute her reasoning from the Akron case, however, that the trimester system of *Roe* must be jettisoned and replaced by her "undue burden" test. *Casey* thus established that the Court would henceforth judge abortion restrictions by whether they posed a "substantial obstacle in the path of a woman seeking the abortion of a nonviable fetus."[15]

In race cases, too, Justice O'Connor has not gone as far as the Court's more conservative justices (Scalia and Thomas) would to ban affirmative action under all circumstances. Instead, she has written the Court's opinions to allow racial preferences if they are "narrowly tailored" to remedy a specific, demonstrable instance of racial discrimination. Her application of "strict scrutiny" (the highest judicial standard in equal protection cases) to set-aside programs for minority contractors had the effect of invalidating such policies, first in *City of Richmond v. J.A. Croson Co.* (involving local set-asides) and then in *Adarand v. Peña* (addressing federal programs). Likewise, in such race-based gerrymandering cases as *Shaw v. Reno* from 1993, she refused to write a sweeping opinion for the Court that would ban majority-minority redistricting per se, but she argued that such districts must satisfy a "compelling state interest." Once more, she applied the highest level of equal-protection analysis, this time to invalidate bizarrely shaped congressional districts in North Carolina drawn solely on the basis of race.

Justice O'Connor's moderately conservative jurisprudence in church-state cases has also shifted both judicial standards and outcomes. In a 1984 case, *Lynch v. Donnelly,* she provided the decisive fifth vote to uphold the display of a Christmas nativity scene sponsored by the city of Pawtucket, Rhode Island. Her concurring opinion reasoned that the First Amendment's Establishment Clause prohibited the government from linking a person's religion to his or her status in the political community, and prevented the state from endorsing or disapproving of religion. She saw no violation by Pawtucket under her two-pronged standard, which allowed wider leeway for state involvement with religion. She expounded upon her reasoning from *Lynch* in another concurrence, this time in the 1985 *Wallace v. Jaffre* decision striking down Alabama's law authorizing a one-minute period of silence in all public schools "for meditation or voluntary prayer." She tried to balance her impermissible endorsement test (which invalidated the Alabama law in her eyes) with the fact that she believed the government could acknowledge religion under the Free Exercise Clause of the First Amendment. In 1997 she garnered a majority in *Agostini v. Felton,* which allowed public-school teachers to provide remedial instruction for children in parochial schools under Title I of the Federal Aid to Elementary and Secondary Schools Act of 1965. Her decision explicitly overturned the Court's twelve-year-old precedent that had ruled oppositely on the same issue.

In the related, but distinct, cases involving the free exercise of religion, Justice O'Connor has also been reliably idiosyncratic. She voted with the majority in 1990 to uphold Oregon's generally applicable ban on controlled substances like peyote, a hallucinogenic drug, that happened to be used by Native Americans as part of their liturgy. While the Scalia-led majority claimed that states did not have to meet a "compelling interest" standard for general laws that might only incidentally touch on religious practices, O'Connor insisted in her concurrence that the high standard of "compelling state interest" remain intact for free exercise cases. Therefore, she dissented from the Court's opinion in 1997 striking down the Religious Freedom Restoration Act, which had embodied Congress's attempt to require federal courts to use the "compelling state interest" standard in free-exercise-of-religion disputes.

Although some observers criticize O'Connor's individualistic approach to constitutional and statutory interpretation as inconsistent and intellectually hollow, admirers find her distinctive reasoning and ability to forge majorities a substantive contribution to moderately conservative jurisprudence. Whatever the assessment, her strategic and crucial votes in closely decided cases cannot be gainsaid. At the close of the 1990s and the twentieth century, Justice O'Connor continues to fulfill with pride her heroine's role as the first female Supreme Court justice. Currently she is the third most senior member of the Court, sitting next to the chief justice, her former classmate and date, Bill Rehnquist. Occasionally, she looks rather small and frail in her large black leather chair when viewed from the audience in the courtroom, but in person she displays a tall, broad-shouldered figure that reflects her years of athleticism. Diagnosed with breast cancer in 1988, she underwent a mastectomy and chemotherapy. The treatments were successful, and she did not miss even one day of oral argument during them, but she understandably recalls the terror she felt at the time of her illness. Moving toward their fiftieth wedding anniversary, the O'Connors speak touchingly about how much they have enjoyed their almost half-century together and how amazed they are at the swift passage of time. Even for an icon, there are human imponderables.

ENDNOTES

1. Personal interview, Washington, D.C., May 14, 1985.
2. Qtd. in Tony Mauro, "Hugs and Wine, Life Beyond the Court," *Texas Lawyer*, May 20, 1996.
3. Qtd. in Andrea Gabor, "Sandra Day O'Connor," in *Einstein's Wife: Work and Marriage in the Lives of Five Great Twentieth-Century Women* (New York: Penguin Books, 1995), p. 274. Gabor's delightful essay, written for a general audience, provides a colorful portrait of Justice O'Connor's life.
4. Qtd. in Barbara A. Perry and Henry J. Abraham, "The Reagan Supreme Court Appointees," in *Great Supreme Court Justices*, ed. William Pederson and Norman Provizer (New York: Peter Lang, 1992), p. 321.
5. Ibid., p. 322.
6. Ibid.
7   Ibid., p. 325.
8. John S. Stookey,"There Is No 'How To Do It Manual' at the Supreme Court," *The Supreme Court Historical Society Quarterly* 19 (1998): 10.
9   Qtd. in John M. Scheb II and Lee W. Ailshie, "Justice Sandra Day O'Connor and the 'Freshman Effect,'" *Judicature* 69 (June/July 1985): 10–11.
10. Joan Biskupic, "Balance of Power," *Washington Post*, July 3, 1998, p. A17.
11. 469 U.S. 528.
12. Personal interview, Washington, D.C., May 14, 1985.
13. See Nancy Maveety's *Justice Sandra Day O'Connor: Strategist on the Supreme Court* (Lanham, Md.: Rowman & Littlefield, 1996), for a cogent and convincing analysis of what she labels O'Connor's "accommodationist" approach to "collective decision-making."
14. 492 U.S. 490.

15.   505 U.S. 833.

CHAPTER FOUR

Antonin Scalia

On a judicial bench that may be the wittiest and most lively in the Court's history, Antonin Scalia is the "King of Comedy." He can toss out one-liners and sardonic quips with the ease of a Las Vegas headliner. His use of them in judicial opinions and at oral argument is now legendary. To a struggling counsel at one of the Court's sessions, he posed a hypothetical set of facts to see how the attorney's argument might apply. The stumped lawyer paused and then, grasping at rhetorical straws, weakly replied, "Your honor, that's not the case before us." Scalia went for the punch line: "No!" he stage-whispered from the bench in mock astonishment. Of course, it wasn't the case at issue, Scalia admitted, but he wanted a response based on the hypothetical he had created. To an interviewer who requested some time with Scalia to discuss his appointment to the Supreme Court and the role his religion might have played in the process, he graciously agreed to discuss the general concept of the so-called "Catholic seat," but added parenthetically, "if that's what I sit in." A lawyer once recognized Justice Scalia pedaling next to him on an exercise bike at a Washington health club. He summoned his courage to enquire, "Excuse me. Are you Justice Scalia?" To which the burly justice replied with a smile, "No, he's thinner than I am." People beyond the Beltway are not immune from the justice's wit. Traveling out West with his family some years ago, he came upon a desk clerk at a motel who, when he saw the name on the credit card, asked if it was pronounced the same as that of the man on the Supreme Court. The justice later reported that he was tempted to reply, "How many Antonin Scalias are there?" For the record, he will tell you that his surname is pronounced, "Skuh-LEE-yuh." To his friends, he goes by the nickname "Nino."

Scalia's facility with language and witticisms may be traceable to a childhood spent with his college-professor father and schoolteacher mother. S. Eugene Scalia, the justice's father, was a Sicilian-born immigrant to the United States who ultimately became a professor of Romance

languages at Brooklyn College. He was deeply devoted to his Roman
Catholic religion and staunchly committed to analyzing literature in its
original language. Translations of the Italian classics were anathema to
him; texts must be read literally to avoid destroying their unique
meanings. One scholar has even argued that the elder Scalia's beliefs may
have shaped Justice Scalia's devotion to literal constitutional interpretation.[1]

Eugene Scalia married first-generation Italian American Catherine
Panaro, and they had their only child, Antonin, on March 11, 1936 in
Trenton, New Jersey. She was a college-educated elementary-school
teacher, whose brother became a county prosecutor and role model for
her young son. The Scalias lived with the Panaros until they moved to
Elmhurst, New York, in Queens, where Antonin attended primary school
P.S. 13 in his middle-class Irish and Italian community.

The next major influence on Scalia's life was his education at St.
Francis Xavier, a Jesuit military prep school in lower Manhattan. His
abundant intellectual and extracurricular talents were already apparent.
He played the French horn, became leader of the marching band, and
landed the lead role in the school's production of *Macbeth*. One high-
school friend commented, "People just competed for second, he was so
superior academically."[2] His lifelong conservatism was also making itself
evident. A former classmate remembers that Scalia "was a conservative
when he was seventeen years old. An archconservative Catholic. He could
have been a member of the Curia [the governing body of the Roman
Catholic Church]. He was brilliant, way above everybody else."[3] His
upbringing in strict pre-Vatican II Roman Catholicism may have also
influenced his pronounced adherence to legalisms in the secular world.[4]

Reinforcing this religious training was his Jesuit undergraduate work
at Georgetown University, the preeminent Catholic institution of higher
learning in the United States. His studies have been described as similar
to a classical European education. All told, the future justice had six years
of Latin and five years of Greek. Just as he had done in high school,
young Scalia graduated first in his class and valedictorian from Georgetown in 1957 and received his degree *summa cum laude*.

With a stellar academic record behind him, he was accepted at Harvard Law School, where he became note editor of the *Harvard Law Review*. Harvard Law School in the late 1950s was still influenced by the judicial philosophy of Felix Frankfurter, the former professor there, who had been appointed to the Supreme Court by Franklin Roosevelt in 1939. The Frankfurtian approach to constitutional interpretation preached judicial restraint and adherence to neutral principles, both of which Scalia would embrace in his own jurisprudence.[5] Once more Scalia's conservatism was obvious to his contemporaries. One of his fellow officers on the law review recalls that Scalia would express his doubts over how much government could do to help people. In 1960 he received his law degree *magna cum laude* and earned a Sheldon Fellowship for postgraduate study and travel in Europe.

While at Harvard, Scalia had met and become engaged to Radcliffe undergraduate Maureen McCarthy. They were married in September 1960. His parents considered it a "mixed marriage" because she was *Irish* Catholic. By 1962 they started their family, which grew to nine children over the next nineteen years. By all accounts, theirs has been a strong union sealed by their mutual devotion to religion and family. In addition to raising her large brood of children, Mrs. Scalia has managed to do volunteer work in hospitals and at church.

Scalia passed the Ohio bar in 1962 and took an associate position at the prestigious Cleveland law firm of Jones, Day, Reavis, and Pogue, where he was to spend the next six years. There he displayed the professional and personal characteristics that were to mark the rest of his career. His colleagues found him intellectually keen, possessed of sharp debating skills, gregarious, and warm. With these compelling qualities, he was adept at forging consensus, but not at the expense of compromising his own views. In fact, he developed a reputation for becoming entrenched in positions once he had staked them out.

Although he made partner at the Cleveland firm, Scalia decided to leave to take an academic position at the University of Virginia Law School in 1967, and he never returned to private practice. Instead, he alternated between government positions and appointments at law schools. In 1971 he became general counsel in the Nixon administration's Office of Telecommunications Policy, where his work helped to facilitate the expansion of the cable television industry. After one year, he received a promotion to the chairmanship of the Administrative Conference of the United States (an independent study group that investigates issues influencing regulatory agencies), where he served until 1974. At that time, he left to become assistant attorney general in charge of the Office of Legal Counsel in the Department of Justice during the presidency of Gerald Ford. In that post, Scalia addressed issues left over from the Nixon years, such as ownership of the former president's papers and the proper scope of the CIA and FBI. He began to develop an abiding respect, which would later be reflected in his judicial opinions, for the power of the presidency.

In 1977 Scalia left government service for a year's stint as a visiting professor of law at Georgetown University and as a "scholar in residence" at the American Enterprise Institute, a conservative think tank in Washington, D.C. There he interacted with colleagues who constituted the right-wing literati, many of them destined to take influential positions in the Reagan administration of the 1980s. Each day they would gather for a brown-bag lunch and discussion of conservative approaches to public policy. Scalia made the next logical step from AEI to a teaching position in 1977 at the University of Chicago Law School, which attracted prominent conservative legal scholars who firmly believed that government should not impinge on a free-market economy. Scalia and his wife bought an old fraternity house near the university to quarter their large and still-growing family. In 1980–81 Scalia took what would be his last position before ascending the bench, a visiting professorship at Stanford Law School in California.

The Reagan administration, which took office in 1981, considered Professor Scalia for the position of solicitor general, but opted instead to nominate him to the United States Circuit Court of Appeals for the District of Columbia. His nomination was remarkably uncontested, with his confirmation hearing before the Senate Judiciary Committee covering only two pages in the record book. In August 1982 he was sworn in to his position on the tribunal that has been called second in importance only to the Supreme Court. His colleagues there described his work habits in language similar to that used by his former partners at the Cleveland law firm. He was charming and good-humored to judges of all ideological stripes and was an able discussant in initial conversations over cases. Nevertheless, when he made up his mind, "he [would] plant his flag and go down in flames with it if he need[ed to]," according to former colleague Abner Mikva. Law clerks for more liberal judges on the D.C. Circuit took to calling him "The Ninopath" for his inflexibility.

Over the next four years, Scalia authored close to 100 opinions. One of the first judges to employ a word processor, he was noted for composing most of his own opinions in his now-famous flamboyant style. His conservative jurisprudence, fashioned over a lifetime, revealed itself in his textualist and originalist approach to constitutional interpretation. The former ties him strictly to the words of the document; the latter to what they meant to the society that adopted them at the Founding. Scalia explains: "I do not believe in the living Constitution, this document that morphs from generation to generation. I favor what some might call the dead Constitution, but I prefer to call it the enduring Constitution."[6] On the appeals court he also displayed his devotion to broad interpretation of executive power, his belief in a limited role for the judiciary, and his loyalty to the separation-of-powers principle. In an opinion widely believed to have been authored by Scalia, a three-judge panel invalidated a key enforcement provision of the so-called Gramm-Rudman-Hollings Act, which was Congress's attempt to balance the ballooning federal budget in the mid-1980s by delegating power to carry out budget cuts to the comptroller general. The panel's reasoning was vintage Scalia, arguing that the comptroller general was removable by Congress and therefore a member of the legislative branch. He could not be granted power to enforce the law, a classic *executive*-branch function, without violating the separation of powers. The Supreme Court later affirmed the ruling.

In addition, Scalia was also on record in judicial opinions and/or scholarly commentaries as opposing affirmative action in the form of racial preferences, questioning the basis for the Supreme Court's fashioning of a right to sexual privacy (including abortion rights and consensual homosexual acts), and taking a narrower view than some of his colleagues about what constituted protected expression under the First Amendment. (In dissent from a decision by the D.C. Court of Appeals, he excluded sleeping in Lafayette Square as a form of protest from his list of protected speech.) Some observers have noted that Scalia's commentaries, both on and off the bench, were decidedly in sync with the Reagan administration's positions on a host of issues.

Whether Scalia deliberately wrote, especially in extrajudicial commentaries, to attract the attention of Reagan and his minions is unknowable. Nevertheless, a full year before Scalia's appointment to the Supreme Court, an unnamed White House official told the *New Republic* that nominating Scalia to the nation's high court made good "political sense." The official exclaimed, "What a political symbol. Nino would be the first Italian Catholic on the Court. He's got nine kids. He's warm and friendly. Everybody likes him. He's a brilliant conservative. What more could you want."[7] Moreover, at age fifty, Scalia was nine years younger than his nearest competitor, Judge Robert Bork, a colleague on the D.C. Circuit and also on Reagan's list of potential nominees. That meant that barring ill health or the unlikely event of an ideological conversion, Scalia could carry the conservative judicial tenets of the Reagan administration well into the twenty-first century.

The opportunity to promote Scalia came unexpectedly in June 1986 when Chief Justice Warren Burger announced his retirement from the bench. According to Reagan's attorney general, Edwin Meese, the president used three criteria in making his decision to fill the Burger vacancy: intellectual and lawyerly capability, "integrity," and "a commitment to the interpretation of the law rather than making it from the bench."[8] Following this trio of guidelines, the president promoted Associate Justice William H. Rehnquist to the center chair, and offered Judge Scalia the ninth seat on the Court at the end of an Oval Office interview with him. Reagan's announcement of his intention to nominate Scalia noted the candidate's "great personal energy, the force of his intellect, and the depth of his understanding of our constitutional jurisprudence [which] uniquely qualify him for elevation to our highest court."[9] When asked at the press conference whether he expected controversy over his nomination in the Senate, Scalia was typically droll: "I have no idea. I'm not a politician."[10]

Indeed, Scalia had no need to worry. While Rehnquist's nomination to chief justice drew all the fire (he would be confirmed by a 68–31 vote after a nasty Senate battle), Scalia found smooth sailing toward his confirmation. His hearings before the Senate Judiciary Committee produced accolades for his professional qualifications and the fact that he would become the first Italian American to sit on the Supreme Court. Senators on the committee engaged in some moderate verbal sparring with Scalia before unanimously agreeing to approve his nomination. On the floor of the full chamber, Scalia was confirmed with nary a negative vote.

Undoubtedly, his meritorious résumé, attractive personality, and ethnic representation propelled his case forward. Perhaps the overriding element in Scalia's favor, however, was the fact that the Republicans controlled the Senate in 1986 by a 53–47 margin over the Democrats. Nevertheless, the Democrats had mounted a vociferous, if unfocused and ultimately unsuccessful, campaign against Rehnquist's promotion. The Rehnquist battle might have drawn some of the fire away from Scalia, leaving the Senate too enervated to take up another political crusade against him. In addition, Reagan's popularity provided support for his nominees. In his own favor, Scalia employed an astute and effective strategy at his hearings by avoiding expansive answers to questions on controversial issues. Finally, many Senators viewed him as simply an ideological clone of Rehnquist, whose seat he would take; they therefore believed he would not alter the balance of the Court's votes.

At the White House on September 26, 1986, Scalia took the oath of office required of all federal employees. Then, smiling broadly, he thanked his wife Maureen "without whom I wouldn't be here, or, if I were here, it wouldn't have been as much fun along the way."[11] At the Supreme Court, he swore a second oath, this one required of all judges, administered by the just-installed Chief Justice Rehnquist.

In a dozen years on the Supreme Court, Justice Scalia has generally exhibited faithfulness to the jurisprudence he enunciated and practiced before coming to the high bench. He has expanded his textualist philosophy in constitutional interpretation to judicial reading of statutes.

Thus, he preaches that judicial interpretation of laws is confined to the language of the statutes themselves and should not include so-called legislative history, which encompasses congressional committee reports, floor speeches, and the general intent of the legislature in passing the law, as divined by the judiciary. In 1992 Scalia labeled legislative history "the last hope of lost interpretive causes, the St. Jude of the hagiology of statutory construction."[12]

Continuing his broad interpretation of executive power, Scalia was alone in dissent from the Court's 1988 majority opinion in *Morrison v. Olson,* which upheld the creation of the independent counsel or special prosecutor. Scalia argued that assigning prosecutorial powers, an executive branch function, to an individual selected by a special panel of three federal judges, and therefore not answerable to the president of the United States, was a patent violation of the separation-of-powers principle. Under that same principle, he was again the author of a solo dissenting opinion the next year in *Mistretta v. United States*. He disagreed with the majority's validation of the United States Sentencing Commission, maintaining that Congress had unconstitutionally delegated legislative power to the Commission, which was granted authority to determine sentencing guidelines to be followed by federal judges. Yet Scalia does not always see a violation of separation of powers, even when a majority of his colleagues do. In the two 1998 cases challenging the line-item veto, the Court struck it down as a violation of the Constitution's requirement that legislation be passed by both houses and presented to the president for his approval or veto in full. Scalia, however, joined by Justices O'Connor and Breyer, saw no distinction between Congress's allowing the president to cancel spending items line by line and Congress's authorizing money to be spent on a particular item at the president's discretion, which has been done since the nation's founding. (This latter point exemplifies Scalia's originalist approach to constitutional interpretation.) His first preference in the line-item veto cases, however, would have been to negate the challenge to the law on procedural grounds that the parties bringing the suit (two interests who claimed they suffered financial injury by President Clinton's veto of spending items affecting them) failed to show that they were harmed by the statute.

Lack of standing to sue (or failure to show harm), is one of the primary elements of judicial self-restraint, whereby the Court can refuse to reach the merits of a case by determining that the plaintiff has failed to demonstrate a concrete individual injury. In fact, the Supreme Court had refused to rule on the substance of the Line-Item Veto Act in 1997 because it argued that the members of Congress who were challenging it did not have standing. Scalia invokes standing frequently as part of his general philosophy that unelected judges should restrain themselves in deference to the democratically elected branches. On whether courts should act to establish rights that may be lacking explicit expression in the Constitution or statutes, Scalia has an equally restraintist answer. He asserts that the proper way to address twentieth-century controversies over abortion, the death penalty, and physician-assisted suicide is to call on legislatures to pass laws supported by the majority of the people. Judicial revision of the eighteenth-century intent of the Constitution violates the document itself. In typically pithy fashion, Scalia has urged in public commentary that "having the Constitution mean whatever five out of nine justices think it ought to mean these days is not flexibility but rigidity." He elaborates: "It is not supposed to be our judgment as to what is the socially desirably answer to all of these questions. That's supposed to be the judgment of Congress, and we do our job correctly when we apply what Congress has written as basically and honestly as possible."[13]

Not surprisingly, some of his most scathing and emotive volleys against judicial imperialism have been fired in abortion cases. His first opportunity to vote on the abortion issue came in the 1988–89 term's highly charged case of *Webster v. Reproductive Health Services*, in which he willingly sided with the narrow majority upholding substantial state restrictions on abortions. His caustic concurring opinion, however, went a step beyond the majority, chastising Justice Sandra Day O'Connor by name for her refusal to overturn *Roe v. Wade* and attacking the rest of the majority for "needlessly . . . prolong[ing] the Court's self-awarded sovereignty over a field where it has little proper business since the answers to most of the cruel questions posed are political and not juridical. . . ."[14]

When the Court accepted *Planned Parenthood of Southeastern Pennsylvania v. Casey* for its 1991–92 term, Scalia understandably thought the case would provide the vehicle for overturning *Roe*. Justice William Brennan, among the majority in *Roe,* had retired in 1990 and was replaced by Bush appointee Justice David Souter, who conservatives hoped would provide another vote to overturn the original 1973 decision establishing a woman's right to abortion on demand in the first three months of pregnancy. Imagine Scalia's anger when Souter formed a plurality with Justices O'Connor and Anthony Kennedy, *reaffirming* the central holding in *Roe* and only slightly mitigating access to abortion in the first trimester. (Justice John Paul Stevens and *Roe*'s author Justice Harry Blackmun supported the plurality, but would have upheld the precedent in its entirety.) Scalia poured out his exasperation in one of the dissents filed in the case, accusing the majority of engaging in "a new mode of constitutional adjudication that relies not upon text and traditional practice to determine the law, but upon what the Court calls 'reasoned judgment' which turns out to be nothing but philosophical predilection and moral intuition."[15]

Scalia's text-based interpretation of the Constitution and statutes has produced numerous opinions decrying the policy of affirmative action to address perceived societal discrimination on the basis of gender and race. In his first term on the Court, he took the Brennan-led majority to task for approving a local transportation agency's promotion of a female employee over a more qualified male colleague. He argued in forceful, sometimes sarcastic terms, that the Court's ruling in *Johnson v. Transportation Agency, Santa Clara County* actually turned Title VII of the Civil Rights Act of 1964 on its head by approving preferential treatment on the basis of gender, which the Act prohibits. In the Court's landmark 1995 ruling in *Adarand v. Peña,* raising the standard that federal set-aside programs for minority contractors must meet under Fourteenth Amendment Equal Protection Clause analysis, Scalia, joined by Justice Clarence Thomas, contributed a concurring opinion that went a step further than Justice O'Connor's majority opinion. Whereas she and her colleagues allowed that a showing of specific racial discrimination (as opposed to general societal bias) could constitute a "compelling state interest" to uphold preferential treatment as a remedy for minority business owners, Scalia argued that under our color-blind Constitution no state interest could ever be so compelling as to permit racial preferences even to atone for past discrimination.

In the highly publicized 1996 case testing the constitutionality of Virginia Military Institute's all-male admissions policy, Scalia found himself in lonely dissent from Justice Ruth Bader Ginsburg's majority opinion striking down VMI's tradition of excluding women from its state-funded program. He returned once more to his textualist and originalist reading of the Constitution, which he noted did not expressly prohibit the long American tradition of government-funded military schools for men. He compared their existence to the policy of sending exclusively men into combat, a tradition upheld by the Court in the 1981 case sanctioning the male-only draft law. In his *VMI* dissent, and his equally angry opposition to the Court's ruling in the 1996 Colorado gay-rights case, voiding a state constitutional amendment that barred local ordinances banning discrimination on the basis of gender orientation, Scalia pointedly accused the majority of advocating the politically correct causes of the legal elite. He happily wrote the Court's opinion in *Lucas v. South Carolina Coastal Council*, however, which many observers saw as the conservative bloc's effort to return property rights to a more even footing with civil rights and liberties.

Although Justice Scalia's consistent attachment to language and tradition usually produces conservative results, it can lead to surprisingly liberal outcomes. In the emotionally charged 1989 flag-burning case, *Texas v. Johnson*, for example, he voted with the five-person majority, led by Justice Brennan, to sanction a political protester's burning of the American flag as protected expression under the First Amendment. Scalia typically cites the case to illustrate that "[t]here's no room in [my] judicial philosophy for my personal political or religious beliefs." Recalling when *Johnson* was handed down, Scalia has said, "I came down to breakfast the next morning and my wife is humming 'Stars and Stripes Forever.' This does not make for a happy camper."[16] His understanding of Fourth Amendment standards regarding unreasonable searches and seizure propelled him to vote with another liberal majority, and even write its opinion, refusing to extend the "plain view" exception to a warrantless search that had discovered stolen stereo equipment. The facts in *Arizona v. Hicks* indicated that a police officer had moved stereo components to reveal their serial numbers, and to Scalia and his colleagues in the majority the traditional doctrine of "plain view" did not obtain if the suspicious object had been moved, even just a few inches, to reveal its incriminating evidence. In another Fourth Amendment case (*National Treasury Employees Union v. Von Raab*), he dissented from the Court's ruling upholding mandatory drug testing for customs employees, finding it an unreasonable search and seizure. In *Vernonia School District v. Acton*, however, he sanctioned random drug-testing by urinalysis for student athletes, citing the reasonableness of the policy and the low expectation of privacy on the part of athletes. Undoubtedly, Justice Scalia would have preferred to find a constitutional formula to limit flag-burning, uphold the conviction of a stereo thief, and discourage drug use among customs officials, but he could not. As he noted in a 1989 law-review article, the rule of law is a law of rules, which must be applied neutrally by the judge regardless of his personal preferences.

His interpretation of the religion clauses of the First Amendment, however, often returns him to the conservative fold. Scalia upheld for a 7–2 Court Ohio's policy of allowing the Ku Klux Klan to erect a cross in front of the state's capitol building, although his opinion focused on the free-speech right of the KKK to expression in a classic public forum. He was livid in dissent from Justice Souter's majority opinion in *Board of Education of Kiryas Joel Village v. Grument*, which struck down New York's creation of a separate school district for a community of Hasidic Jews. Scalia repeatedly argued that the Founding Fathers had created a constitutional tradition of religious toleration that the Court had violated with its extreme separationist rulings. Nevertheless, religious toleration has its limits, as demonstrated by Scalia's ruling in the 1990 Oregon case in which Native Americans challenged the state's prohibition of peyote use. Because the hallucinogenic drug is a staple of Indian liturgy, the plaintiffs argued that the Oregon law violated their free-exercise-of-religion rights under the First Amendment. Scalia wrote for the six-person majority that the Oregon law could be sustained because it was not directly aimed at religious practices. Its general applicability had only an "incidental" impact on religion.

The Oregon case also demonstrates Scalia's support of legislative pronouncements unless they impinge on constitutional principles as he perceives them. Federalism, with a general emphasis on state power, receives high priority in his jurisprudence. Thus, he wrote the Court's 1997 opinion striking down the unfunded mandates imposed on the states by the Brady Gun-Control Law and voted with the 1995 majority that invalidated the Gun-Free School Zones Act as reaching beyond the Congress's commerce power and impinging on state prerogatives. Not surprisingly, Scalia voted, in dissent, to uphold the right of twenty-two states to establish term limits for their members of Congress.

Scalia's overall voting profile on the Court is generally considered conservative. He has found an ideological soulmate in Justice Thomas, with whom he voted 82 percent of the time in non-unanimous cases in 1997–98. During that same term, of the fifteen cases (out of ninety-one) decided by a 5–4 vote, the most frequent voting bloc included Chief Justice Rehnquist and Justices Kennedy, O'Connor, Scalia, and Thomas.[17] Scalia's dual, and sometimes contradictory, characteristics of promoting consensus but holding firm to positions have also been displayed on the high court. The above litany of majority opinions indicates that he can write for colleagues and command a majority. Nevertheless, he also has earned a reputation for solo dissents, often written in a patented acerbic, occasionally mean-spirited, style. Some observers initially questioned his breadth of influence if the latter pattern were to continue, but Judge Alex Kozinski of the Ninth Circuit Court of Appeals maintains that the sheer number and weight of Scalia's ideas will ensure his influence over the length of what may prove to be an extended tenure on the Court.

While "The Ninopath" can slice an opposing justice's opinion to ribbons, he maintains a playful side that allowed him to appear on stage as an opera extra in eighteenth-century costume (including powdered wig and knee breeches) with friend and colleague Justice Ginsburg. Despite their judicial differences, she enjoys their friendship because, she says quite simply, he makes her laugh. He has also been spotted leading sing-alongs at Court receptions, where he belts out "oldies" to piano

accompaniment with gusto. But he cannot be dismissed as a ham or
judicial comedian; his philosophy, intellect, and personality will remain
forces to be contended with for as long as he sits on the Supreme Court
(in whatever he wishes to call his seat!).

ENDNOTES

1. For a brilliant analysis of Justice Scalia's approach to interpreting the Constitution, and of the impact that his father and Roman Catholicism might have had on that approach, see George Kannar, "The Constitutional Catechism of Antonin Scalia," *Yale Law Journal* 99 (April 1990): 1297–1357. An insightful book-length study of Scalia's jurisprudence is David A. Schultz and Christopher E. Smith's *The Jurisprudential Vision of Justice Antonin Scalia* (Lanham, Md.: Rowman & Littlefield, 1996).

2. Qtd. in Ruth Marcus and Susan Schmidt, "Scalia Tenacious After Staking Out a Position," *Washington Post*, June 22, 1986, p. A16.

3. Qtd. in Irvin Molotsky, "Judge with Tenacity and Charm," *New York Times*, June 18, 1986, p. A31.

4. Kannar, p. 1314.

5. Peter B. Edelman, "Justice Scalia's Jurisprudence and the Good Society: Shades of Felix Frankfurter and the Harvard Hit Parade of the 1950s," *Cardozo Law Review* 12 (June 1991): 1799–1815.

6. Qtd. in Richard Carelli, "A Speechless Scalia Puts Unlikely 'Spin' on His Conservatism," *Washington Post*, May 23, 1997, p. A27.

7. Barbara A. Perry and Henry J. Abraham, "The Reagan Supreme Court Appointees," in *Great Justices of the Supreme Court*, ed. William Pederson and Norman Provizer (New York: Peter Lang, 1992), p. 332.

8. Qtd. in Barbara A. Perry, "The Life and Death of the 'Catholic Seat' on the United States Supreme Court," *The Journal of Law and Politics* 6 (Fall 1989): 87.

9. Qtd. in "President's News Conference on Resignation of Chief Justice," *New York Times*, June 18, 1986, p. A30.

10. Ibid.

11. Qtd. in Ruth Marcus, "Rehnquist, Scalia Take Their Oaths," *Washington Post*, September 27, 1986, p. A4.

12. Qtd. in Joan Biskupic, "Scalia Sees No Justice in Trying to Judge Intent of Congress on a Law," *Washington Post*, May 11, 1993, p. A4.

13. Qtd. in Glen Johnson, "Deciding Abortion, Suicide Issues Is Duty of Congress, Scalia Says," *Washington Post*, March 3, 1998, p. A7.

14. 492 U.S. 490.

15. 505 U.S. 833.

16. Qtd. in Carelli, p. A27.

17. Joan Biskupic, "Balance of Power," *Washington Post*, July 3, 1998, p. A17.

CHAPTER FIVE

Anthony M. Kennedy

Anthony Kennedy has a genuine dramatic flair. He once participated in a moot court based on the *dramatis personae* of a Shakespearean play, took a role in the Washington, D.C. production of Ibsen's *Peer Gynt* (along with his colleagues Justices Ginsburg and Breyer), and delivered lectures dressed as James Madison. Beyond the realm of playacting, however, he also knows when a dramatic turn of phrase can capture the profundity of his work as a Supreme Court justice. Prior to announcing his crucial vote in the closely decided 1992 Pennsylvania abortion case *Planned Parenthood of Southeastern Pennsylvania v. Casey*, he excused himself from a reporter, saying, "I need to brood. . . . It's a moment of quiet around here to search your soul and your conscience."[1] He is also an eloquent advocate of the Court he serves and the rule of law in American society. In his earnest temperament, inspiring eloquence, and bespectacled visage, he is the very model of the judge/lawyer/professor he has played in real life.

Life began for Anthony McLeod Kennedy on July 23, 1936, in Sacramento, California, the home of his father, Anthony J. ("Bud") Kennedy, and his mother, Gladys ("Sis") McLeod Kennedy. Bud Kennedy was a successful lawyer and lobbyist at the California state legislature. His wife Sis, a 1928 graduate of Stanford University, worked as a teacher and then a secretary in the California Senate, where she met her future husband, whom she married in 1932. The Kennedys had three children (two boys and a girl); Anthony was the middle child. Their home in Sacramento, a white, two-story colonial built by Mr. Kennedy, was a hub of political, civic, and social activity. Among the elder Kennedy's associates were California Governor Earl Warren, the future chief justice of the United States, and other prominent politicians.

Thus, from his early childhood young Anthony Kennedy circulated among California's most celebrated citizens. While still in grade school, he began serving as a page in the California Senate, a position arranged by his parents. When his father was trying cases, he would sometimes invite his son to accompany him to court. The future justice estimated that he had witnessed ten jury trials before he was even out of high school.

At McClatchy High School in Sacramento, Anthony routinely made the honor roll and won awards from the California Scholarship Federation. He reportedly experienced a remarkably trouble-free boyhood that included regular service as an altar boy at his Roman Catholic parish church. As one of his friends described Kennedy's reputation, "When we were growing up, if any of us were going to do something naughty, Tony would go home."[2] Kennedy used to joke with his friends that his father, in a fit of affectionate despair, had offered to pay him $100 if just once he would do something requiring his parents to come pick him up at the local police station! The youngster never collected on the dare.

Kennedy always assumed that he would attend Stanford like his mother and become a lawyer like his father, and Kennedy did indeed follow in his parents' footsteps. As an undergraduate majoring in history and political science, the future justice continued his outstanding academic career at Stanford. He was particularly captivated by constitutional law, and his professor for that class described him as brilliant. Kennedy completed his graduation requirements in three years, but his father apparently thought his son was too young to enroll immediately in law school, so young Tony spent a year at the London School of Economics. Upon his return in 1958, he received his B.A. degree from Stanford, where he was elected to Phi Beta Kappa. He then attended Harvard Law School, from which he obtained his degree, *cum laude*, in 1961.

After a six-month stint in the California Army National Guard, he began his practice of law in the prestigious San Francisco firm of Thelen, Marrin, John & Bridges, but within two years he was back in Sacramento to assume the law practice of his father, who had died suddenly of a heart attack in 1963. For four years he worked in the solo practice and then became a partner in the firm of Evans, Jackson, and Kennedy, where he remained until 1975. He assumed his father's lobbying duties; but, described as an intellectual, Kennedy seemingly disliked the flesh-pressing and glad-handing required of such work in the state capital. Eventually, he found an outlet for his more academic interest in the law when the dean of McGeorge School of Law at the University of the Pacific offered him a part-time teaching position. Just as in his student days, he thrived in the classroom and would often amaze his own students by lecturing for three hours on constitutional law without referring to a note.

In 1963 Kennedy had married Mary Jeanne Davis, a Stanford graduate and elementary-school teacher, and they eventually had three children, Justin, Gregory, and Kristin, all of whom are Stanford graduates. The Kennedys raised the children in the Sacramento home built by their paternal grandfather, where Anthony had spent his own happy childhood.

Like Bud Kennedy, the future justice was a Republican, if not a particularly active one. Nevertheless, in the early 1970s he was asked to serve on a commission to draft a tax-limitation initiative known as Proposition 1 for Ronald Reagan, then the governor of California. Although the ballot proposition failed in 1973, a similar proposal passed in 1978, fomenting a taxpayer revolution in the Golden State. Moreover, Kennedy had impressed the Reagan camp with the constitutional expertise he brought to the commission. When an opening became available on the U.S. Court of Appeals for the Ninth Circuit in 1975, Reagan recommended Kennedy to President Gerald Ford, who appointed the thirty-eight-year-old Californian to the bench, making him the youngest federal appellate judge in the country.

Kennedy would spend the next thirteen years on the Ninth Circuit, watching it expand from thirteen active judges when he joined it in 1975 to twenty-three jurists during the presidential administration of Jimmy Carter from 1977 to 1981. Carter filled the expanded circuit with his appointments, rendering it the most liberal in the nation. In this ideological context, Judge Kennedy was known as a conservative, but one more in touch with the Gerald Ford than the Barry Goldwater wing of the Republican Party. As a jurist, Kennedy was thorough, respectful of precedent, and open-minded. He simply refused to confine himself in any jurisprudential straitjacket.

Of the 430 opinions that Judge Kennedy wrote on the Ninth Circuit, one of the most important was in *Immigration and Naturalization Service v. Chadha*, a 1980 case in which he ruled that the "legislative veto," allowing one or both houses of Congress to block executive-branch decisions, was an unconstitutional violation of the separation of powers. The U.S. Supreme Court affirmed his decision in a 1983 ruling. Another 1980 Kennedy opinion attracted more headlines at the time he wrote it. In *Beller v. Middendorf* he asserted that U.S. Navy regulations prohibiting homosexual conduct were constitutional. He did not dismiss the possibility that the Constitution might afford a right to sexual privacy in civilian contexts. Five years later Kennedy angered women's rights groups by overturning a ruling that would have mandated that the state of Washington compensate female employees millions of dollars for their "comparable worth" to men in similar jobs. In *AFSCME v. State of Washington*, Judge Kennedy argued for the Ninth Circuit that the discrepancy between pay for men and women in Washington was *not* the demonstrable result of gender-based discrimination.

Judge Kennedy was marking a dozen years on the federal appellate bench when Justice Lewis F. Powell, Jr., unexpectedly announced his retirement from the U.S. Supreme Court in June 1987. No commentator failed to report the ramifications for the tribunal's future direction. Indeed, Powell had played a pivotal role as the tie-breaking vote in cases determining the Court's interpretation of constitutional law on abortion, affirmative action, and separation of church and state. He was neither consistently liberal nor conservative, but had swayed the Court's decisional outcomes from one ideological camp to another by virtue of his "swing vote."

President Ronald Reagan and his advisors badly misjudged the impact of "swing seat" politics on the appointment process when they nominated Judge Robert Bork of the U.S. Circuit Court of Appeals for the District of Columbia to fill Powell's position. Unquestionably qualified by virtue of his intellect, education, and experience, he was, nevertheless, stridently conservative in his long "paper trail" of judicial opinions and scholarship. With the Democrats in control of the Senate, the Bork hearings before the Judiciary Committee were a bloodbath. Bork's commitment to a jurisprudence of original intent of the Founding Fathers appeared rigid and was fair game for being portrayed as beyond the mainstream of contemporary judicial philosophy. Moreover, Bork's personal appearance and demeanor seemed as suspect as his ideology. His devilish beard and sometimes turgid academic discourse did not endear him to senators, liberal interest groups, or the public. Nor did his detailed, lecture-like answers to every conceivable question posed to him by the Senate Judiciary Committee. No careful observer of the drama over filling the "swing seat" could have been surprised by the ultimate denouement that saw Bork's nomination go down in a resounding 42–58 defeat in the Senate.

Reagan's vindictive nomination of Judge Douglas Ginsburg, also of the D.C. Circuit Court of Appeals, rubbed salt in the appointment battle wounds. Ginsburg was a young devotee of the conservative "Law and Economics Movement." Although he lacked the paper trail of his predecessor Bork, a long fight over his nomination loomed in the Senate. Only the startling disclosure of his past marijuana use, both as a student and as a law professor, saved the country from another wrangle over the nomination of a perceived extremist for Powell's crucial seat.

In his third attempt to fill the vacant spot on the nation's high court, President Reagan turned to Anthony Kennedy, announcing his nomination on November 11, 1987—five months after Justice Powell had made public his departure from the bench. In selecting Kennedy, Reagan described him as a popular judge who had established a record on the Ninth Circuit that was fair but tough in applying the law. The president also labeled Kennedy "a true conservative . . . who believes that our constitutional system is one of enumerated powers."[3]

By virtue of his moderately conservative judicial record, his moral propriety, and his pleasant appearance and personality, Kennedy appeared to be the antithesis of Robert Bork or Douglas Ginsburg. There was no doubt that Kennedy's decisions during his long tenure on the appellate bench produced conservative results, but his opinions seemed more narrowly crafted than Bork's. Thus Kennedy could plausibly argue in his written responses to a standard Judiciary Committee questionnaire that "[l]ife tenure is a constitutional mandate to the federal judiciary to proceed with caution, to avoid reaching issues not necessary to the resolution of the suit at hand, and to defer to the political process."[4] On the issue of judicial philosophy, he added, "It's somewhat difficult for me to offer myself as someone with a complete cosmology of the Constitution. I do not have an overarching theory, a unitary theory of interpretation. . . . I think if a judge decides a case because he or she is committed to a result, that it destroys confidence in the legal system."[5]

On December 14, 1987, the opening day of the Kennedy hearings, the Supreme Court split 4–4 on a case involving the constitutionality of an Illinois law requiring minors wanting abortions to notify their parents. The tie vote only heightened the urgency of filling Justice Powell's seat on the Court that had been vacant since June. Anthony Kennedy's record and performance at his confirmation hearings convinced the Senate Judiciary Committee that he was the perfect choice to fill the vacancy. The committee report, which unanimously endorsed Kennedy's nomination, described him as "open-minded, fair, and independent," and as possessing "the truly judicious qualities that Justice Lewis Powell embodied."[6] Accepting the committee's unqualified approval, the full Senate voted on February 3, 1998 to confirm Kennedy's nomination 97–0. He took two oaths of office, one at the White House and one at the Court, on February 18, 1988, and started work immediately on the Court's term that was already half over. Fortunately, his thirteen years as a federal judge on an appellate court prepared him for the rigors of work at the Supreme Court, so there was no "freshman effect" causing him to maintain a low profile.

By 1989 Kennedy's voting record and several majority opinions already distinguished him from Justice Powell. Instead of functioning as a vote that balanced the liberal and conservative blocs by siding with one or the other from case to case (as had Justice Powell), Kennedy's vote began to tip the balance most often in favor of the conservatives. In the abortion realm, for example, Kennedy voted with the 5–4 majority in *Webster v. Reproductive Health Services* to allow states the right to impose substantial new restrictions on abortion. Kennedy also arrived at a conservative result on the matter of the right to privacy and the drug-testing issue. In *Skinner v. Railway Labor Executives* and *National Treasury Employees v. Von Raab*, he wrote both majority opinions for the

Court's constitutional sanction of the federal government's efforts to create a drug-free workplace.

In the area of affirmative action, Justice Kennedy began to distance himself most fundamentally from Justice Powell. In early 1989 Kennedy voted with the 6–3 majority in *City of Richmond v. J.A. Croson Co.*, invalidating a local set-aside law in Richmond, Virginia, that channeled 30 percent of public-works funds to minority-owned construction companies. He also cast his vote with the narrow 5–4 majorities that reached conservative results in two additional 1989 affirmative-action/employment-discrimination cases in *Martin v. Wilks* and *Wards Cove Packing v. Atonio*.

In just his first full term on the high court, Kennedy's most notable contribution to the tribunal's more conservative tack in employment discrimination cases was his 1989 majority opinion in *Patterson v. McLean Credit Union*, which upheld the use of the 1866 Civil Rights Act for claims of discrimination at the initial hiring stage, but barred use of the statute for claims of on-the-job bias.

In church-state matters Kennedy revealed a conservative accommodationist stance, particularly in simultaneous 1989 rulings in *Allegheny County v. Greater Pittsburgh A.C.L.U.* on Christmas-season displays, sponsored by city and county governments in Pittsburgh. He dissented from a decision declaring that a Nativity scene, unaccompanied by any more secular symbols of the season, amounted to an unconstitutional endorsement of the Christian faith. He found himself in the majority, however, when the Court permitted a Hanukkah menorah to be displayed next to a Christmas tree.

Another 1989 First Amendment case, this time in the free-expression realm, found Kennedy uncharacteristically joining a liberal decision in *Texas v. Johnson*, which declared via Justice William Brennan's opinion that burning the American flag as a political protest is a form of protected symbolic speech. Kennedy was uncomfortable enough with his vote in the majority that he penned a concurring opinion to explain that "[t]he hard fact is that sometimes we must make decisions we do not like. We make them because they are right, right in the sense that the law and the Constitution, as we see them, compel the result."[7] Kennedy's vote and rationale for it signaled that in some instances he might behave more like the justice he replaced, Lewis Powell, judging each decision on a case-by-case basis.

The voting line-ups on the Supreme Court in the 1990s bear witness to that assessment of Kennedy's role. In church-state cases, he perplexed conservatives with his 1992 majority opinion in *Lee v. Weisman,* arguing that nonsectarian prayers at public-school graduation ceremonies violated the First Amendment's Establishment Clause. Justice Antonin Scalia's dissent for four members of the Court labeled the decision "senseless" and "unsupported in law."[8] Kennedy also joined the majority two years later in *Board of Education of Kiryas Joel Village v. Grumet,* which invalidated New York's creation of a separate school district for a community of Satmar Hasidic Jews so that their handicapped and special-education children would not have to attend public schools. In the 1995 case of *Rosenberger v. University of Virginia,* however, he argued for the narrow five-person majority that Rosenberger's free-expression rights to publish a student-run Christian magazine trumped the University's argument that to provide him with funds raised from student-activities fees would violate the Establishment Clause.

In cases involving the free exercise of religion, Kennedy joined the majority in the 1990 landmark decision of *Employment Division, Department of Human Resources of Oregon v. Smith,* upholding the state's prohibition on liturgical use of peyote (a hallucinogenic drug) by Native Americans. Justice Scalia's opinion held that the First Amendment's Free Exercise Clause did not ban "generally applicable" laws that have only an "incidental" effect on religious practices. In response to the decision, Congress passed the Religious Freedom Restoration Act of 1993 that required laws to meet a higher standard, known as a "compelling state interest," if they impinged on religious practices. Justice Kennedy, applying the reasoning from *Smith,* produced the Court's opinion in its unanimous 1993 decision, *Church of the Lukumi Babalu Aye v. Hialeah,* striking down the Florida city's ban on animal sacrifices, which all nine justices viewed as a direct attack on the Cuban-American Santeria sect's religious practice of killing animals. Nevertheless, in 1997 Kennedy penned the opinion for a 6–3 Court invalidating the Religious Freedom

Restoration Act in *City of Boerne v. Flores*. He and his colleagues in the majority viewed the act as a congressional usurpation of the Court's power to determine the parameters of constitutional protection of religion and an intrusion on the states' authority to make laws.

Kennedy's fealty to the separation of powers (dividing the roles of the three branches of government according to constitutional mandates) and federalism (assigning powers to national and state levels of government again by constitutional directives), was evident in *Flores*. His loyalty to the twin principles of American constitutionalism had also been present in his 1995 deciding vote in *United States v. Lopez*, invalidating a federal law, which banned guns near local schools, and restricting Congress's commerce power. Yet in that same term he sided with the interests of the national government, rather than the states, when he cast another deciding vote, this time in *U.S. Term Limits v. Thornton*, striking down state laws limiting the terms of their members of Congress. His concurring opinion emphasized the "distinctive character" of the federal government and added, "There can be no doubt, if we are to respect the republican origins of the Nation and preserve its federal character, that there exists a federal right of citizenship, a relationship between the people of the Nation and their National Government, with which the states may not interfere."[9]

In matters of race, Justice Kennedy has remained fairly consistent with his initial tendency to vote with the conservatives. He wrote for a unanimous Court in the 1992 case of *Freeman v. Pitts* that racially segregated schools resulting from private choice, not state action, are not subject to constitutional remedies. That same year, in a voting case from Alabama, he held for the majority in *Presley v. Etowah County Commission* that two counties were not required under the Voting Rights Act of 1965 to abolish their new system of road management that had reduced the effective power of newly elected black commissioners. Kennedy's opinion two years later in *Holder v. Hall* ruled for a 5–4 Court that the size of a governmental body cannot be challenged under the Voting Rights Act as diluting the influence of minority voters because no legal standard exists for determining the "fair" number of representatives. He followed that decision with the 1995 redistricting ruling in which he concluded for another 5–4 majority that race could not be the "predominant factor" used in drawing majority-minority districts. Justice Kennedy could also be found with the narrow majority holding in 1995's *Adarand v. Peña* that federal set-aside programs favoring minority contractors must be held to the highest "compelling state interest" standard.

As a Supreme Court justice, Anthony Kennedy has also remained consistent in his conservative analysis of criminal rights, which he developed on the lower appellate court. In matters of privacy and gender, however, he has raised eyebrows for reaching liberal results. The abortion issue produced voting blocs along three different fault lines in the 1992 *Casey* decision. There were four votes to overturn *Roe v. Wade*: Chief Justice Rehnquist and Justice Byron White (the two dissenters in *Roe* when the case was handed down in 1973), and Justices Scalia and Thomas. Two justices in the five-person majority wished to uphold *Roe* in its entirety: Justice Harry Blackmun (*Roe*'s author) and Justice John Paul Stevens. Justices Kennedy, Souter, and O'Connor formed a three-person plurality whose opinion upheld the "central holding" of *Roe* while abolishing its cumbersome trimester system for determining when women have the right to terminate their pregnancies. In its place they substituted the "undue burden" test, which allowed state restrictions on abortion even in the first trimester as long as they did not pose "substantial" obstacles to a woman seeking such a procedure. The trio's stunning opinion emphasized the Court's need to uphold precedent as a means of protecting its legitimacy; overturning the two-decades-old decision, around which many in society had ordered their lives, would irreparably damage the Court's authority, according to the plurality's reasoning.

Romer v. Evans, decided by the Court in 1996, was a closely watched case that touched on the contentious issue of gay rights. After several cities in Colorado passed ordinances banning discrimination based on sexual orientation, Colorado voters adopted an amendment to the state's constitution precluding such protection of homosexuals or bisexuals. Led by Justice Kennedy's opinion, a 6–3 Court invalidated the Colorado amendment on the grounds that it violated the federal Fourteenth Amendment's Equal Protection Clause by disqualifying one class of persons from seeking governmental safeguards. Even under the lowest level of Equal Protection analysis (the "rational relation" test), the state amendment was fatally flawed in both its application and justification. It singled out one class of persons, denied them the prospect of legal protection, and seemed motivated by animosity toward the class rather than a legitimate governmental purpose.

On the last day of the Court's 1997–98 Term, Justice Kennedy announced the majority opinion in *Burlington Industries, Inc. v. Ellerth*. By the same vote (7–2), and with the same justices in dissent (Thomas and Scalia), the Court ruled in this case and *Faragher v. City of Boca Raton* that an employer is vicariously liable for actionable sexual harassment perpetrated by a superior, subject to an affirmative defense by the employer that considers the reasonableness of his conduct and that of the victim. Kennedy and Souter, who wrote in *Faragher*, expanded legal recourse for victims of sexual harassment, thus filling a gap in federal statutory law left unaddressed by Congress.

Aside from his substantive contributions to cases in the last decade of the twentieth century, Justice Kennedy, like Justice Powell before him, has often provided the pivotal swing vote in closely decided cases. In the fifteen cases determined by one vote in the 1997–98 term, Kennedy was in the majority in all by three. Overall, he was in the majority 93 percent of the time, more than any other justice in 1997–98.[10] He thus replicated a pattern he had established in the previous several terms, leading at least one analyst to label the high tribunal "the Kennedy Court."[11]

To some observers, Kennedy evinces an infuriating inconsistency. They say he twists in the wind until he fastens onto an idiosyncratic reason for deciding a case. To others, he is a thoughtful jurist who steadfastly refuses to embrace a results-oriented ideology; he simply analyzes each case on its own merits. Which assessment to apply may depend on the assessor's own ideological predilections. On one point, however, Anthony Kennedy's position is clear and unwavering: his commitment to the rule of law, the legal profession, the role of the judge, and the American constitutional cosmos.[12] Anyone who witnessed his compelling challenge to the United States to revitalize its civil society in the wake of the tragic 1995 bombing of the Alfred P. Murrah Federal Building in Oklahoma

City knows that his understanding of America's most admirable traditions is profound and indisputable.

ENDNOTES

1.   Qtd. in Joan Biskupic, "When Court Is Split, Kennedy Rules," *Washington Post*, June 11, 1995, p. A14.

2.   Qtd. in Barbara A. Perry, "The Life and Death of the 'Catholic Seat' on the United States Supreme Court," *Journal of Law and Politics* 6 (Fall 1989): 89.

3.   Qtd. in "Reagan Nominates Kennedy to Fill Court Seat," *Congressional Quarterly Weekly Report* 45 (1987): 2830.

4.   Qtd. in Nadine Cohodas, "Kennedy Finds Bork an Easy Act to Follow," *Congressional Quarterly Weekly Report* 45 (1987): 2989.

5.   "Hearing Excerpts: Kennedy on the Issues," *Congressional Quarterly Weekly Report* 45 (1987): 3130.

6.   U.S. Senate Committee on the Judiciary, *Report on the Nomination of Anthony M. Kennedy to Be an Associate Justice of the United States Supreme Court*, 100th Cong., 2d sess., 1988, pp. 23, 27.

7.   491 U.S. 397.

8.   505 U.S. 577.

9.   514 U.S. 779.

10. Joan Biskupic, "Balance of Power," *Washington Post,* July 3, 1998, p. A17.

11. Jeffrey Rosen, "The Agonizer," *New Yorker*, November 11, 1996, p. 84.

12. An eloquent statement of Kennedy's views on these subjects can be found in the text of his speech "Law and Belief," delivered at a meeting of the American Bar Association, August 2, 1997, and available online at www.usis-israel.org.

CHAPTER SIX

David H. Souter

An unlikely venue and occasion provide the perfect opportunity to view the public persona of David Souter, the man who was called the "stealth nominee" and "Justice Fuzzy" upon his appointment to the Supreme Court of the United States in 1990 because he was so little known in political and judicial circles at the time. In March 1996 Souter and his colleague Justice Anthony Kennedy appeared before a House of Representatives Appropriations Subcommittee, ostensibly to testify about the Court's budget for the next fiscal year. This now-annual ritual features some pro forma discussions of budget line items for the Court, and then members of the subcommittee turn to more substantive questions regarding the judiciary, which the justices answer with surprising frankness. Justice Souter, a slightly built man, attended the 1996 subcommittee hearing dressed in a pin-striped, charcoal-gray suit, starched white shirt, and sedate dark blue tie. At age fifty-seven, Souter wore his thinning, salt-and-pepper hair neatly trimmed. His face was marked by a perpetual five-o'clock shadow and revealed deep lines when he smiled. Deferring to his senior colleague, Souter referred to himself as "junior counsel" and declined when asked if he would like to add to Justice Kennedy's opening statement. After letting Kennedy answer most of the initial questions, Souter then made a few comments so that he would not appear to be "a bump on a log," as he put it. Self-deprecating humor, delivered in Souter's distinctive New England accent, has become one of his trademarks. Yet his twinkling eyes and benign facial expression turned as flinty as the granite hills of his beloved home state, New Hampshire, when the topics raised by the House committee struck a serious chord with him. Suddenly the terse Souter turned loquacious, even eloquent, defending the American jury system with raw passion as he described his early career as a prosecutor and then a trial judge, when he developed an admiration for jurors' abilities to comprehend complex arguments in criminal trials. And in relating a story about a stubborn grand jury, which refused to indict a suspect in a case Souter wanted to prosecute, he told of his eventual support for the "cantankerous" citizens who set themselves as counterpoints to the power of the state.

When the committee turned to its final topic of allowing television cameras in courtrooms, including the Supreme Court, Souter's response potently combined his dry humor, formidable character, and certainty of purpose: "The day you see a camera coming into our courtroom, it's gonna roll over my dead body!" He elaborated by saying that his experience with televised sessions at the New Hampshire Supreme Court, where he served seven years, proved to him that cameras have a detrimental effect on the judicial process. The 1996 hearing illustrated that six years after his appointment to the nation's highest court, Souter's personality and opinions are not in the least "fuzzy."[1]

Yet the 105th justice of the Supreme Court of the United States remains something of a mysterious paradox. Although he has followed the American pattern of many a small-town boy made good, he has done so with a lifestyle that is *sui generis*. Born on September 17 (Constitution Day), 1939, in Melrose, Massachusetts, David Hackett Souter was the only child of Joseph Alexander and Helen Adams Hackett Souter. The Souters spent considerable time at the home of David's maternal grandparents in Weare, New Hampshire, a small, rural community just a few miles from Concord, the state capital. At age eleven, with his grandparents now deceased, young David and his parents moved to sedate Weare and settled in the ramshackle family farmhouse, a move necessitated by Joseph Souter's heart condition. David's father enjoyed the slower-paced life of a bank officer in Concord. Mr. Souter passed away in 1976 and Mrs. Souter eventually moved to a retirement home, but David Souter was still living in the family's Weare homestead when President George Bush plucked him from obscurity to place him on the nation's highest court in 1990. When his schedule allows time away from Washington, he continues to retreat to the secluded life of the small house that is stuffed with books, records, and memories.

By educational background alone, Souter seemed a worthy candidate for the U.S. Supreme Court. He attended public elementary schools and Concord High School, where he was elected president of the National

Honor Society and was voted by his classmates as "most literary," "most sophisticated," and "most likely to succeed" upon graduation in 1957. David then entered Harvard College, where he joined the irreverent Hasty Pudding club and majored in philosophy, writing his senior honors thesis on the jurisprudence of Oliver Wendell Holmes. When he graduated *magna cum laude* and Phi Beta Kappa from Harvard in 1961, a group of his friends presented him with a scrapbook filled with headlines they had invented to represent the future they predicted for him: one read "David Souter Nominated to Supreme Court." Knowing that he seemed destined for the prestigious judgeship, some of his friends took to calling him "Mr. Justice Souter."

The next step toward that destiny came with his selection as a Rhodes Scholar, which allowed him to attend Magdalen College, Oxford to study law and philosophy for two years. His friends from that era remember that he accepted with ease the antiquated mores of the medieval university. His regular attendance at chapel set him apart from his Rhodes colleagues; and while they traveled in Europe during the long vacations, Souter stayed behind to study. His fellow Rhodes Scholars also recall that he was a staunch defender of the United States and was offended by anti-American comments. Still, he had already developed the high art of conversation and was considered an entertaining dinner companion, despite his preference for formality and privacy.

After returning to the United States in 1963, Souter enrolled at Harvard Law School. A photograph from those years depicts young Souter dressed in a tuxedo and enjoying a cigar at a formal banquet. He performed well in his classes but did not make the law review. His proctorship of a freshman dormitory, where he was on call twenty-four hours a day, was a drain on his time but introduced him to problems unknown in his previously sheltered life. At his hearings before the Senate Judiciary Committee in 1990, Souter told the wrenching story of having to advise a freshman and his girlfriend after she became pregnant. The future justice did not reveal the nature of his advice to the distraught couple, but he used the event as an illustration of his exposure to the "real world." While attending law school, he dated Ellanor Stengel Fink, a student at Wheaton College, but neither the relationship with her nor his dating experiences with other women over the ensuing years resulted in marriage. Friends say that Souter is really wedded to the law and his career in it.

Graduating from Harvard in 1966, Souter returned to his beloved home in Weare and began his legal career in private practice with the firm of Orr & Reno in Concord. He found the general litigation practice there unrewarding and turned to the public sector. In 1968 he joined the staff of the New Hampshire attorney general as an assistant attorney general in the criminal division, with assignments at both the trial and appellate levels of the state court system. Warren Rudman, who was destined to become a U.S. senator and who would play a key role in supporting Souter's eventual U.S. Supreme Court nomination, became attorney general of New Hampshire in 1970 and promoted Souter to be his top aide as deputy attorney general. The two became close friends and professional colleagues. Rudman described Souter as the most talented member of his staff, with a skill for producing cogent, logical writing based on a thorough knowledge of case law. Moreover, the future senator was taken with Souter's warmth, good humor, and genuine concern for people. Rudman has reported that Souter's charm is especially attractive to children, with whom he communicates easily and genuinely. He is especially close to his young goddaughter.

Rudman, upon resigning in 1976, persuaded Governor Meldrim Thomson to name Souter as his successor. In his two-year service as state attorney general, from 1976 to 1978, Souter personally argued several controversial religion cases. In one, he defended Governor Thomson's questionable order to fly the American and state flags at half-staff on Good Friday. He also supported in court the state's attempts to prosecute residents who, for religious reasons, covered up the state motto—"Live Free or Die"—on their license plates. The state was unsuccessful in the litigation of both cases.

Nevertheless, Souter's service was rewarded with a judicial appointment to the state Superior Court in 1978. He served on that trial court for five years, riding circuit around New Hampshire's ten counties and encountering every kind of case that typically can come to a tribunal of general jurisdiction. He developed a judicial reputation as fair but unsympathetic toward criminal defendants, and he acquired his admiration, expressed so eloquently at the 1996 congressional hearing, for juries. In 1983 New Hampshire Governor John Sununu, who would become President Bush's chief of staff, named Souter to the New Hampshire Supreme Court. On the five-person tribunal, Souter established himself as the intellectual leader and became a commanding presence at oral arguments. The high court of a small state tends not to hear cases of major constitutional import, but in a case challenging sobriety checkpoints, Souter dissented from his court's opinion that they were unconstitutional under the New Hampshire Constitution. Eventually, the U.S. Supreme Court agreed with Souter's point of view in upholding such checkpoints in a Michigan case. While on the Superior Court, a serious romance evolved between Souter and a woman attorney he knew from the attorney general's office; when the relationship ended, he was said to be crushed.

Souter led a full and busy life outside the courtroom, however. He was a fixture at the local Episcopal church, where he assisted elderly parishioners. Inspired by his aunt, Harriet Bartlett, who had a successful career as a medical social worker in Boston, he served on the Board of Trustees of Concord Hospital from 1972 to 1985, including a six-year stint as the board's president. In addition, he was an overseer of the Dartmouth Medical School, and he pursued his love of history as a trustee of the New Hampshire Historical Society. Although somewhat reclusive in his penchant for solitary pursuits, such as reading and listening to classical music, he also liked to escape to the outdoors and climb the White Mountains of his adopted state. By the time of his next promotion, Souter had become famous among his colleagues for his endearing preferences for driving dilapidated cars and eating the same lunch (yogurt or cottage cheese with a whole apple—core and all) day after day.

In 1987 the Senate refused to confirm President Ronald Reagan's nominee, Robert Bork, for a seat on the U.S. Supreme Court. Reagan's next nominee, Douglas Ginsburg, had to withdraw when word spread in the media that he had smoked marijuana. Senator Warren Rudman could hold his tongue no longer; he phoned Reagan's chief of staff, Howard Baker, and recommended David Souter for the still-vacant seat on the high court. White House aides spoke to Souter and were reportedly impressed, but Reagan nominated Anthony Kennedy on the advice of his attorney general, Edwin Meese.

By early 1990 a position had opened on the U.S. First Circuit Court of Appeals, and Rudman was back on the phone with the White House, this time with George Bush's chief of staff, John Sununu, the former governor of New Hampshire who had placed Souter on the state Supreme Court. The Senate approved Souter's nomination unanimously, and Judge Stephen Breyer, then chief judge of the First Circuit, swore him in on May 25, 1990. He had yet to write an opinion for that court when Justice William J. Brennan, Jr., unexpectedly announced his retirement from the Supreme Court on July 20, 1990. At age eighty-four Brennan was in declining health, but he had remained a vigorous member of the Court and a formidable creator of majority coalitions through its 1989–90 term. Indeed, he had fashioned majorities (albeit slim ones) for the dwindling liberal bloc in his last contentious cases involving flag-burning and affirmative action. Yet Justice Brennan, who had served with distinction since 1956, suffered a slight stroke early in the summer of 1990, and his physician urged him to accept the inevitable. He reluctantly announced his retirement, citing the incompatibility of the burdens of the Court with his fragile health.

Now Senator Rudman went to work to earn the ultimate prize for his friend and protégé. He phoned Sununu and then President Bush and told him, "Mr. President, you have just appointed this man [Souter] to the First Circuit Court of Appeals and he can easily be confirmed for the Supreme Court. I can guarantee you that he has no skeletons in his closet, and he's one of the most extraordinary human beings I've ever known."[2] Rudman then alerted his friend that the White House would probably contact him.

Bush was grateful for Rudman's recommendation but made no commitments to him over the phone. Nevertheless, the president publicly vowed to make quick work of the selection process for Brennan's replacement. The administration had compiled a list of potential nominees during Bush's first year in office; it included then-Solicitor General Kenneth Starr and three other federal appeals court judges (Edith Jones,

Lawrence Silberman, and Clarence Thomas). White House Counsel C. Boyden Gray tracked Judge Souter down by phone in his Concord office on the weekend after Brennan announced he was leaving the Court and asked Souter to come to Washington on the very next day for a conversation with the president. Souter was skeptical of the process and his chances to land a nomination. Moreover, as he noted some years later, he was perfectly happy with his life in New Hampshire and thrilled to have been named to the U.S. Court of Appeals. Friends encouraged him to accept the request for an interview at the White House, if for no other reason than it would generate a lifetime's worth of interesting anecdotes. Souter acquiesced on the condition that he would answer no questions from the administration about his views on particular issues, especially abortion. A supportive Rudman drove Souter to the Manchester airport for his flight to Washington, and even loaned his old friend $100 when the future justice discovered that he had only $3 in his wallet.

The short list of potential nominees had already been narrowed to Souter and Edith Jones by the time the former arrived at the White House to meet with administration staffers and the president himself. Bush and Souter had a productive discussion—two traditional New Englanders comparing notes and philosophies. In Souter, the president saw a perfect nominee for the times: a brilliant jurist who represented the best of American virtues while exhibiting no vices or known controversial positions on judicial issues. He had written over 200 opinions while on the New Hampshire Supreme Court, but they reflected a state docket rather than the divisive federal constitutional issues that reach the U.S. Supreme Court. A computer search of law-review articles turned up a sole example of Souter's published work, which consisted of a eulogy for a New Hampshire judge. If Robert Bork had been foiled by his own extensive paper trail of conservative commentaries on virtually every major constitutional debate of the day, Souter was indeed the "stealth nominee," named for the military aircraft whose unique design enables it to deflect radar. His very obscurity was the overwhelming deciding factor in his favor and gave him the nod over Judge Edith Jones.

With a stunned candidate at his side, President Bush announced Souter's nomination on the same day he met him for the first time, a mere seventy-two hours after Brennan had signaled his retirement from the bench. The president stressed that Souter was "a remarkable judge of keen intellect and the highest ability, one whose scholarly commitment to the law and whose wealth of experience mark him of first rank." Refusing to speculate on Souter's positions on specific issues, Bush tried to position him as a conservative with the coded language that Souter had "a keen appreciation of the proper judicial role rooted in fundamental belief in separation of powers and the democratic principles underlying our great system of government."[3] Bush's chief of staff, John Sununu, who as governor of New Hampshire had named Souter to the state's Supreme Court, remarked, "What [Souter] says and does is what he is. No pretense, no surprises."[4]

When called to the podium at the presidential news conference, Souter humbly thanked President Bush and then offered the media these few words, in rather jumbled syntax: "If it were possible for me to express to you the realization that I have of the honor which the president has just done me, I would try, and I would keep you here as long tonight as I had to do to get it out."[5] With that, he reserved any further comment for his confirmation hearings. Bush took a few more questions from reporters, but successfully dodged all the inquiries calling for Souter's specific stance on issues. The news conference ended, and in the privacy of the White House Bush offered Souter a drink to calm him and called the nominee's mother to tell her the astonishing news. In the weeks leading up to his hearings before the Senate Judiciary Committee, Souter was subjected to media probes into his personal life that were painful for the nominee and fruitless for the journalists. For an intensely private man, the scouring of his life and habits (especially his bachelorhood) was nearly more than he could bear. In fact, he reportedly told his friend Senator Rudman that if had known how vicious the process would be, he would not have let the senator propose his name.

Rudman defended the man he describes as being like a "very special younger brother" to him. Introducing Souter on the first day of hearings before the Senate Judiciary Committee, Rudman angrily declared, "It is remarkable that there are some people here in Washington who view a man who has a single-minded dedication to his chosen profession, the law, and possesses great qualities of humility, graciousness, frugality, charity, reverence to his faith and to his family is somehow regarded as an anomaly and somehow out of touch with life."[6] Rudman later wrote, "If David Souter is odd, our society is in big trouble."[7] But Rudman need not have worried; his old friend from New Hampshire impressed the committee with the very qualities Rudman had always admired in him. Souter's nomination cleared the Judiciary Committee by a vote of 13–1, with only Senator Edward Kennedy (D.–Mass.) casting a negative vote. The full Senate was equally favorable, approving Souter by a vote of 90–9. The new justice was sworn in on October 9, 1990, and began work almost immediately on the fall term, which was already underway.

During his entire first term on the high bench, Justice Souter was inundated with the work that awaited him in an atmosphere, in a city, and in a context that were totally unfamiliar to him. Historically, freshmen justices take a reserved role while they acclimate to their new surroundings, but Souter was even less visible than most. He wrote only nine majority opinions, none of which was considered of major significance, and penned just two concurring and two dissenting opinions. His votes aligned him with the Court's conservative bloc, but he had the highest level of agreement (89 percent) with Justice Sandra Day O'Connor, considered a moderate conservative.[8] In criminal justice cases, he continued his tendency from his days on the New Hampshire courts to side with the government as opposed to defendants. Observers noted that his predecessor, Justice Brennan, a champion of criminal rights, would surely have voted in the opposite direction from his replacement. Conservatives also hailed Souter's decisive vote in *Rust v. Sullivan*, which upheld the constitutionality of regulations prohibiting federally funded family-planning clinics from discussing abortion with their clients.

After a refreshing summer in Weare, Souter returned to the Court for his second term in the fall of 1991 with much more confidence in his ability to handle the job at an institution he utterly revered. His charm, warmth, and good humor had won him friends among the Court's close-knit staff. He settled into a routine in his chambers, where, perhaps to recall his roots, he hung a portrait of Harlan Fiske Stone (also from New Hampshire), who had served as associate justice and then chief justice earlier in the century. Visitors to Souter's office have noted that it is unusually dark, with no desk lamps to cast additional light; and, reflecting the justice's traditional work habits, he writes in calligraphic longhand rather than succumb to the modern convenience of a word processor. Souter also settled into a routine in oral arguments, often asking probing but polite questions of counsel. Once, at a 1994 oral argument, his strong New England brogue betrayed him. He was attempting to ask a counsel about the "flaw" in his argument. It was a reasonable question, to be sure, except that with Souter's accent, the question asked for the "floor" in the attorney's contention. The baffled counsel paused and then wisely asked for a clarification on Souter's query regarding the "floor" in his position. The justice realized the source of confusion and then sheepishly apologized for what he called his "regional accent," prompting laughter from those assembled in the courtroom.

After arriving at the Court, Justice Souter struck up a friendship with his predecessor, the retired Justice Brennan, who maintained chambers in the Court building. A poignant photograph of the two shows Justice Souter tenderly supporting a feeble Justice Brennan by the arm as they attended the 1993 funeral of Justice Thurgood Marshall. We may never know the extent of Justice Brennan's jurisprudential influence on his successor, but Justice Souter's moving eulogy to his friend "Bill" at the latter's funeral in 1997 spoke volumes about their close personal relationship. The reserved, formal Yankee judge revealed how the gregarious Irish jurist would embrace him in a warm bear hug, call him "pal," and always make him feel "great" during visits to his chambers. Tongue in cheek, Justice Souter also reminisced about how Justice Brennan, a renowned master at mustering majorities on the nine-person Court, taught him "how to count to five."[9]

The majority that Souter helped fashion in the 1992 case of *Planned Parenthood of Pennsylvania v. Casey* was reminiscent of Brennan-led factions in the past. Holding the votes of *Roe v. Wade*'s author, Justice Harry Blackmun, and Justice John Paul Stevens for part of the decision, Souter was influential in coauthoring a plurality opinion with Justices O'Connor and Kennedy that reaffirmed what the trio called the "central holding" of *Roe*, that a woman may choose to terminate her pregnancy based on the prerogative of a constitutionally protected personal liberty. The three centrist justices argued that the 1973 *Roe* precedent was such an accepted part of society in 1992 that the Court should protect the core of the ruling and its own legitimacy by reaffirming the heart of the decision. Souter, Kennedy, and O'Connor abandoned *Roe*'s trimester system of determining when a woman had an unfettered right to choose an abortion, however, and substituted the "undue burden" test for it. A state limitation on access to abortion poses such a burden, in the plurality's definition, when it "has the purpose and effect of placing a substantial obstacle in the path of a woman seeking an abortion of a nonviable fetus."[10]

Needless to relate, conservatives, particularly members of the pro-life movement, were devastated that Souter had not provided the fifth vote to overturn *Roe v. Wade*. In addition, the "stealth nominee" from New Hampshire, who was supposed to offer "no surprises," seemed to be relishing an escalated war of words with his conservative colleague Antonin Scalia, with whom he sparred in several opinions.[11] In First Amendment Establishment Clause cases, Souter began to take the lead on the separationist side. He wrote for the Court in *Board of Education of Kiryas Joel School District v. Grumet* that the state of New York could not constitutionally carve out a separate school district for a village of Satmar Hasidic Jews so that they would not have to send their special-education/handicapped students to secular public schools. Scalia's dissent in the 1994 case repeatedly criticized Souter by name, violating the Court's long-standing tradition of not singling out individual justices for reproach (especially when they are representing the Court as an institution in a majority opinion). Souter's passionate dissent in *Rosenberger v. University of Virginia* also argued the separationist cause by defending the university's decision not to fund a student-run Christian magazine with proceeds from a student-activities fee.

Under the Free Exercise Clause of the First Amendment, Souter wrote a concurrence in the 1993 case of *Church of the Lukumi Babalu Aye v. Hialeah*, agreeing with the Court's ruling in favor of striking down a Hialeah law against animal sacrifice practiced by the Cuban-American Santeria sect. But Souter added that the Court should return to its previously more liberal test for upholding free-exercise claims in virtually all cases. Thus, he was in dissent from the Court's 1997 ruling in *City of Boerne v. Flores* overturning the Religious Freedom Restoration Act, which was Congress's attempt to force the Court to do just what he had argued in *Hialeah*.

By the 1994–95 term, when the second Clinton appointee, Justice Stephen Breyer, joined the Court, Souter could most often be found in civil rights and liberties cases aligning with the more liberal wing of the Court. Because that wing usually consisted of a four-person minority (Souter, Stevens, Ginsburg, and Breyer), Souter was frequently in dissent, as he was in race cases like *Adarand v. Peña* and *Missouri v. Jenkins II*, where the Court reached a conservative outcome. In majority-minority districting cases, concerning voting districts created on the basis of race to ensure minority representation, he was again on the losing side, supporting such race-based reapportionment remedies throughout the 1990s. And crucial federalism cases were no different; Souter was on the dissenting side in *U.S. v. Lopez* and *Printz v. United States*, as the Court's more conservative majority struck down congressional exercises in gun control as overstepping the bounds of federal power.

In 1997–98 Justices Souter, Breyer, and Ginsburg voted together 62 percent of the time in non-unanimous cases. Indeed, on the Court's very last day of that term, Souter announced the majority opinion he had written for the four liberals, plus Chief Justice Rehnquist and Justices O'Connor and Kennedy, in *Faragher v. City of Boca Raton*, a much-anticipated decision in which the Court held that an employer is vicariously liable for actionable sexual harassment caused by a supervisor, but subject to an affirmative defense looking to the reasonableness of the employer's conduct as well as that of the victim. Usually the justice who announces the opinion for the Court will state if there were any dissents in the case and who wrote them. In the 7–2 *Faragher* decision Justice Thomas wrote a stinging dissent joined by Justice Scalia, but Justice Souter neglected to mention that fact. Only after Justice Stevens, presiding over the Court in place of the absent chief justice, prompted Souter with a rhetorical question, "There was a dissent in that case, wasn't there?" did he smile and admit, "There was indeed." An innocent oversight or a deliberate snub of the two most conservative members of the Court? The inscrutable David Souter had struck again!

ENDNOTES

1.   The proceedings were televised on *America and the Courts*, C-
        SPAN, March 30, 1996.

2.   Warren B. Rudman, *Combat: Twelve Years in the U.S. Senate*
        (New York: Random House, 1996), p. 162. Rudman's book
        contains an entire chapter on his friendship and professional
        association with David Souter.

3.   Qtd. in "President Bush's Announcement and Excerpts from
        News Conference," *Washington Post*, July 24, 1990, p. A12.

4.   Qtd. in R.W. Apple, Jr., "Sununu Tells How and Why He
        Pushed Souter for Court," *New York Times*, July 25, 1990, p.
        A12.

5.   Qtd. in "President Bush's Announcement," p. A12.

6.   Rudman, p. 152.

7.   Ibid., p. 155.

8.   Scott P. Johnson and Christopher E. Smith, "David Souter's First
        Term on the Supreme Court: The Impact of a New Justice,"
        Judicature 75 (February/March 1992): 240.

9.   David H. Souter, "In Memoriam: William J. Brennan, Jr.," 111
        Harvard Law Review (November 1997): 1.

10.   505 U.S. 833.

11.   See David J. Garrow's insightful analysis of Souter's evolving
        jurisprudence in "Justice Souter: A Surprising Kind of
        Conservative," *New York Times Magazine*, September 6, 1994,
        p. 36.

CHAPTER SEVEN

Clarence Thomas

Clarence Thomas has observed that biographers, while they can portray their subjects as saints or devils, can never peer into their souls and know what life was really like for them. Such is the challenge for anyone chronicling the biography of the second African American to sit on the Supreme Court of the United States. Yet Thomas frequently speaks publicly of the triumphs and tragedies in his life's story and how he reacted to them. He remembers his youth, when he "was just a little black kid in a world that is far away—both in space and time" from the world he inhabits now, "cloistered in the judiciary."[1]

Indeed, Thomas's ascendence to the highest tribunal in the land could never have been predicted from the dire circumstances of his birth and early childhood years. He was born on June 23, 1948, just south of Savannah, Georgia, in a poverty-stricken segregated community of 500 black residents, which took its name, Pin Point, from the erstwhile plantation that had occupied marshy land on the banks of the musically titled Moon River. After the Civil War, the plantation was divided among the freed slaves who had once been employed there. In the twentieth century their descendants eked out a bare subsistence by processing shellfish.

Clarence was the second of three children (he had an older sister and a younger brother) born to Leola Williams and M.C. Thomas. For the first seven years of his life, the future justice lived in a one-room shack with dirt floors and no plumbing. When he was two years old, his father abandoned the family, leaving his mother with two children and a third one on the way. She attempted to support her family by working as a maid and obtaining clothes for her children from their Baptist church's clothing drives. At the age of seven, when their substandard home burned down, Clarence and his brother were sent to Savannah to live with their grandfather, Myers Anderson, and his wife Christine.

Anderson, a devout Catholic, an active member of the NAACP, and a resourceful businessman (he was a self-employed deliverer of fuel and ice), sent Thomas to a parochial school, St. Benedict the Moor, which was staffed by strict but supportive nuns. Although the school was racially segregated, Thomas notes that its emphasis on discipline and achievement was determinative in his life. He never fails to acknowledge and thank the nuns who taught him there, and he invited them to his investitures for both the U.S. Court of Appeals and the U.S. Supreme Court. Thomas also credits his grandparents with instilling in him good manners and respectful behavior. He recalls that "any report that we threw trash on the ground, failed to greet an adult properly, or engaged in any improper behavior resulted in immediate sanctions."[2] Other institutions, like the local library, nourished his love of reading and helped him to escape into an imaginary world far from the strictures of the Jim Crow South in the 1950s. In later years Thomas has grieved over the loss of what he calls the "ameliorating structures" of his old neighborhood. The small businesses are gone, having succumbed to urban decay; his Catholic elementary school is closed, and its convent tellingly converted to a halfway house; and the branch library stands empty.

In 1964, the year the Civil Rights Act was signed into law, Thomas's grandfather, planning a vocation in the priesthood for his grandson, withdrew him from the all-black parochial high school he was attending and sent him to an all-white Catholic boarding school in Savannah, St. John Vianny Minor Seminary. Although subject to the racist attitudes of some of his classmates, Thomas made excellent grades and played on the school's football team. He attended classes six days a week and retired by 9 p.m. each night. After Clarence's graduation from high school in 1967, Grandfather Anderson sent him to Immaculate Conception Seminary in northwestern Missouri to continue his study toward the priesthood. Although Thomas was not the only black student there, he suffered from the poor race relations extant at the school. A bigoted, insensitive remark by a fellow student about the assassination of Martin Luther King, Jr., in April 1968 changed Clarence's mind about a religious vocaton: he would *not* become a priest.

The decision bitterly disappointed his grandfather, but Clarence eventually enrolled at the College of the Holy Cross in Worcester, Massachusetts, which had begun an active recruitment program for minority students. Thomas was a devoted student who "was always in the library," according to one friend. He majored in English literature because, as he explains it, he had to obliterate the vestiges of his childhood language. He had grown up speaking Gullah, a mix of English and African dialects native to the black inhabitants of the Sea Islands off the Carolina and Georgia coasts. He recalls that he did not necessarily want to major in English but thought it essential to do so in order to learn how to speak and write properly.

Despite his devotion to studies, Thomas found time to participate on the track team, work in the school cafeteria, and volunteer to help the poor in Worcester once a week. He also assisted in founding the Black Student Union at Holy Cross. Thomas seemed haunted by racial isolation and academic pressures and admitted later that he had seriously considered dropping out of college. Yet, fearful that he would be drafted for service in the Vietnam War, Thomas stayed at Holy Cross and graduated ninth in his class in 1971 with honors in English. Another reason that Thomas may have decided to stay in school was his introduction to Kathy Ambush, a pretty coed at a nearby Catholic women's college. A few days after they met, Thomas told a friend that he was in love with Kathy, and they were married in Worcester the day after Clarence's college commencement. Their son Jamal was born two years later.

After receiving his undergraduate degree, Thomas won a scholarship to Yale University Law School through its affirmative-action program. In his courses, he received mostly passes on Yale's grading scale of honors, pass, low pass, and fail. He appeared to fit in academically and socially, but years later described his "rage" and loneliness at feeling snubbed by whites who viewed him as an affirmative-action token and ignored by blacks with more elite backgrounds. In his third year of law school he interviewed with law firms but again felt he was treated differently because of his race. He had hoped to return to his home state of Georgia to work against the injustices he had witnessed in his childhood, but was rebuffed by the major law firms there. He still recalls the bitterness that welled up inside him at the time when all he had to show for his efforts were the "barren husks of rejection letter after rejection letter."[3]

Rescuing him from his frustration and despair was a young, charismatic lawyer and politician, John C. Danforth. Then attorney general of Missouri, Danforth offered Thomas a position in his office as an assistant attorney general. The fact that Thomas at the time was not a Republican and had even voted for George McGovern, the hapless Democratic candidate for president in 1972, did not matter to Danforth, a rising star in the Republican Party. After his graduation from Yale in 1974, Thomas passed the Missouri bar and began putting in long hours in the attorney general's office. He describes those years as ones of continued economic hardship, as he struggled to make ends meet while supporting his wife and young son. One morning, while walking to work, he discovered a wallet, stuffed with bills totaling almost $700—representing more than his monthly take-home pay. He wrestled with his conscience over what to do with the windfall, but ultimately returned the lost billfold to its rightful owner, knowing that the moral lessons dictated by his scrupulous grandparents required that he do so. In the short run, his honesty went unrewarded by the wallet's owner, who treated Thomas with suspicion and ingratitude.

With Danforth's election to the Senate in 1977, Thomas took a job as an attorney with the Monsanto Company, a chemical manufacturer in St. Louis. His duties included ensuring that pesticides produced by the company met federal guidelines. In 1979 he moved to Washington, D.C. and became a legislative assistant to Senator Danforth on the condition that he *not* be assigned to civil-rights issues. His resentment toward the tokenism of affirmative action, bred during his days at Yale, combined with his grandfather's lessons on self-sufficiency and independence, had moved Thomas into a small circle of black conservatives who rejected the dependency allegedly fostered among blacks by the welfare state.

Thomas's conservative ideas quickly brought him to the attention of the Reagan administration, which was always looking for qualified conservative minorities. In 1981 Thomas was appointed assistant secretary for civil rights in the United States Department of Education. He openly stated that minorities must succeed by their own merit and that affirmative action programs and civil rights legislation do not improve living standards. In 1982 he became the chairman of the United States Equal

Employment Opportunity Commission, which was designed to enforce antidiscrimination laws that cover race, gender, and age in the workplace. Thomas served two consecutive terms as chairman, despite having previously sworn that he would never work at the EEOC. Over his eight-year tenure there, Thomas shifted the focus of the commission from large class-action law suits to individual cases of discrimination.

Yet as Thomas's professional career rocketed upward, his personal life was disintegrating. He and his wife Kathy separated in 1981 and were divorced in 1984; Thomas was granted custody of his son. In 1983, his beloved grandfather died. Three years later, however, he met Virginia Lamp, then a spokesperson for the U.S. Chamber of Commerce, at a conference. They were married five months later, with Jamal serving as best man for his father at the ceremony. Now married over a decade, he introduces his wife Virginia at public events as the "most wonderful human being in the world" and his "best friend."

In 1990 President George Bush appointed Thomas to the U.S. Court of Appeals for the Washington, D.C. Circuit, a well-known professional stepping stone to the Supreme Court. Thomas filled the seat left vacant by the resignation of Robert Bork, the unsuccessful nominee to the Supreme Court in 1987. In Thomas's brief eighteen-month stint on the appeals court, he wrote only twenty opinions, none of which involved major constitutional issues. He also voted, but did not contribute written opinions, in approximately sixty decisions. Hewing to a clear conservative line, Thomas tended to defer to the government in cases brought by all parties except businesses. Thus, litigants with civil and criminal rights appeals, challenges under environmental laws, antitrust enforcement cases, and labor grievances generally found an unsympathetic ear in Judge Thomas.[4]

In June 1991 an aging, frail Thurgood Marshall announced his retirement from the Supreme Court, where he had served as the tribunal's first and only black member since his historic appointment by President Lyndon Johnson in 1967. President George Bush faced a thorny political dilemma in choosing Marshall's successor. African Americans saw the Marshall position on the Court as the "black seat," in the tradition of seats reserved for Catholics, Jews, and geographic constituencies in the past.

Yet Bush had voiced his opposition to racial quotas in employment and education, so he could hardly nominate a justice solely because of his or her race. In addition, he had riled the conservative wing of his party by failing to continue the Reagan legacy in many policy areas; therefore, he could ill afford to widen the chasm by nominating a politically moderate, let alone a liberal, minority.

In anticipation of the departure of either Marshall or Justice Harry Blackmun, both of whom were octogenarians, Bush's advisers had composed lists of possible nominees. When Marshall preceded Blackmun in retirement, the Bush administration placed a heavy emphasis on minority and women candidates. Joining several Hispanic, and two women, federal judges on the list was Clarence Thomas, who clearly was being groomed for the appointment by his elevation to the U.S. Court of Appeals in Washington. Moreover, Thomas's publicly articulated conservative stands on some of the most contentious issues on the country's judicial agenda, combined with his age (he was just forty-three), made him a most attractive possibility. With the urging of Vice President Dan Quayle and White House Counsel C. Boyden Gray, President Bush announced, on July 1, 1991, Thomas's nomination to replace Thurgood Marshall. In proclaiming his choice, Bush argued that "the fact that he [Thomas] is black has nothing to do with the sense that he is the best qualified at this time."[5] Throughout the confirmation process, the president would repeat this claim in an unsuccessful attempt to protect his reputation as an opponent of racial quotas. Very few students of the Court believed that Thomas, with his limited experience, would have been chosen had he been white. The American Bar Association's Committee on Judiciary confirmed this view when it subsequently rated him as merely "Qualified," because of his lack of legal credentials. Nonetheless, as Thomas humbly and poignantly accepted the nomination on the lawn outside Bush's tony Kennebunkport, Maine summer estate on a sunny New England afternoon, neither he nor the president could have imagined just how stormy the confirmation process would become.

Civil-rights interest groups portrayed varied reactions to the Thomas nomination. The NAACP's board was nearly unanimous in its 49–1 vote against the appointment of Thomas, whom they accused of being oblivious to institutional racism in his opposition to affirmative action and welfare policies. The National Bar Association (a group of black attorneys) narrowly opposed the Thomas nomination. The National Urban League decided to express its neutrality on the appointment, and the National Council of Black Lawyers, a liberal interest group, announced their opposition to Thomas's promotion to the Supreme Court. Only the Southern Christian Leadership Conference, among the major civil rights organizations, supported him.

After an undistinguished hearing before the Senate Judiciary Committee, during which Thomas refused to be drawn into lengthy discussions of his conservative record and writings, the Committee tied 7–7 in its vote on the nominee, and his name headed to the full Senate without the endorsement of the committee. Before the Senate's vote, however, journalists leaked a sensational story about an FBI report that the Judiciary Committee had received in which University of Oklahoma law professor Anita Hill accused Thomas of sexually harassing her when she worked at the EEOC. The committee summoned Hill, an African-American graduate of Yale Law School, who described in shocking detail the nature of the alleged harassment in front of a transfixed, national television audience. The nominee was recalled to respond to the charges, which he denied absolutely with an obvious contempt for the process that he described as "a high-tech lynching for uppity blacks," evoking the fatal end that many black men met in the South before antilynching laws went into effect. Despite the improbable spectacle, Thomas was confirmed by the Senate 52–48, the closest Supreme Court confirmation vote of the twentieth century. Seven years after his humiliating ordeal, Justice Thomas still spoke of it in bitter terms, describing the Hill hearings as "just a plain whipping" from which he still had not fully healed.[6]

On October 23, 1991, an emotionally battered but determined Clarence Thomas was sworn in as an associate justice of the Supreme Court in a ceremony on the White House lawn. He has admitted that he was not a student of the Court before he began serving on it. In fact, he had never attended an oral argument session at the high court. His biggest surprise upon arriving at the imposing building was how civil and respectful his fellow justices were toward him. Thomas quotes one of his new colleagues as saying, "You are here now, and what you do here is all that matters."[7] Although he has described the workload as "voracious" and challenging, and claims that it took several years for him to feel completely comfortable with it, Justice Thomas embraced a relatively visible role in opinion-writing from the beginning. Not surprisingly, he quickly settled into a voting bloc that includes his conservative soulmates Justice Antonin Scalia and Chief Justice William Rehnquist. In the 1997–98 term, for example, Thomas and Scalia voted together 82 percent of the time in non-unanimous cases. Observers have noted that Thomas is usually a silent participant in oral argument, sitting through the entire 1993–94 term of the Court without posing a single question to the counsel arguing before the bench. At most, he asks but a handful of queries per term. He traces his reticence to advice imparted by his grandparents: "My grandmother told me, 'You can't talk and listen at the same time.' If I wanted to talk a lot, I'd be on the other side of the bench."[8]

In general, the civil-rights community was correct in predicting that Thomas would often oppose their interests. His unwillingness to interpret broadly the Constitution or statutes clearly applies to matters of race. In the 1992 case of *Presley v. Etowah County Commission* he joined the majority in holding that the Voting Rights Act of 1965 did not forbid two Alabama counties to change their systems of road management in such a way that they reduced the effective power of newly elected black commissioners. Similarly, he joined the Court in 1993's *Shaw v. Reno* decision, holding that state officials must present a "compelling" reason to justify "bizarre" congressional districts drawn to contain a majority of blacks or Hispanics. One year later, concurring in *Holder v. Hall*, he urged passionately that the Voting Rights Act does not require, nor could it constitutionally, that race be considered affirmatively in districting. When *Shaw*'s progeny arrived at the Court in 1994–95, Thomas again voted with the majority, this time ruling in *Miller v. Johnson* that when race is the "predominant factor" in establishing legislative districts, they should be presumed unconstitutional.

Thomas's most controversial opinions in race cases came at the end of the 1994–95 term. In *Missouri v. Jenkins II* the justices ruled by a 5–4 majority that a federal judge had improperly attempted to integrate the public schools of Kansas City, Missouri by ordering massive expenditures in an attempt to attract students from surrounding suburbs. Thomas's stunningly emotive concurring opinion declared, "It never ceases to amaze me that the courts are so willing to assume that anything that is predominantly black must be inferior."[9] The same day as the Court handed down *Jenkins*, it announced its opinion in *Adarand v. Peña*, which determined that judges must apply "strict scrutiny" to federal affirmative-action programs, thus jeopardizing all such plans. Not surprisingly, given his previous record against affirmative action as a remedial public policy, Thomas voted with the narrow 5–4 majority. He also joined Justice Scalia's concurrence, which went beyond Justice O'Connor's more moderate controlling opinion, to declare that the government can *never* constitutionally justify racial discrimination against whites as a remedy for past discrimination against minorities.[10]

In one of his first criminal rights cases on the Supreme Court, Thomas followed the tendency he manifested on the Court of Appeals in siding against an inmate who argued that a prison guard had used excessive force against him and thus violated his Eighth Amendment right against cruel and unusual punishment. In dissent from the Court's 1992 opinion in *Hudson v. McMillian*, Thomas argued that the guarantees of Amendment VIII should not, by judicial fiat, be codified to regulate the behavior of prison authorities throughout the country. His opinion seemed especially ironic in light of his comment at the first set of his 1991 confirmation hearings that he would gaze out his window at prisoners coming to the courthouse in Washington and think to himself, "There but for the grace of God go I." Yet Thomas wrote for a unanimous Court in the 1995 case *Wilson v. Arkansas* that the Fourth Amendment's proscription of unreasonable government searches and seizures may be triggered by a police officer's unannounced entry into a home. Per Thomas's opinion, the Court accepted the common-law principle that law enforcers should knock and announce their presence before bursting into a suspect's home. Nevertheless, Thomas left it to lower courts to determine exceptions to the common-law rule when countervailing law-enforcement considerations might prevail. But Thomas returned to his hard line against the aggrieved individual in the Court's 1997 5–4 decision in *Kansas v. Hendricks*, which upheld the state's Sexually Violent Predator Act. Thomas argued for the Court that the act's procedures for civil commitment and its definition of "mental abnormality" in the context of violent pedophilia satisfied "substantive" due-process requirements.

In two criminal-rights cases handed down at the end of the 1997–98 term, Justice Thomas authored both majority opinions for closely split decisions. He joined the more liberal justices—Souter, Ginsburg, Stevens, and Breyer—in ruling that a punitive forfeiture is forbidden under the Eighth Amendment's excessive-fine provision if the forfeiture is "grossly disproportional to the gravity" of the offense. In this case of *United States v. Bajakajian*, an individual successfully challenged the federal government's efforts to keep $357,000 that he had tried to carry out of the country to pay a legal debt in Syria. By law, persons carrying more that $10,000 into or out of the United States are required to declare it. Thomas joined with his more usual lineup of Justices Scalia, Kennedy, O'Connor, and Chief Justice Rehnquist to rule in *Pennsylvania Board of Probation and Parole v. Scott* that illegally seized evidence can be used against defendants in *parole* hearings even if the Fourth Amendment would prevent their use at a *trial*. Justice Thomas's drafting of these two majority opinions, with two such remarkably varied voting blocs, signaled an increase in his ability to cement the crucial five votes needed to decide a case.

Beyond decisions involving the Bill of Rights, one of Thomas's most visible opinions came in the 1995 case *U.S. Term Limits, Inc. v. Thornton*, in which he wrote the lead dissent for Rehnquist, O'Connor, and Scalia. That alignment of four would have upheld the actions of twenty-two states, which by that time had passed laws imposing term limits on their members of Congress. The majority, however, ruled that such limits would violate the uniformity of the federal system; such a major shift in the constitutional order could only be effected through an amendment to the U.S. Constitution. Thomas's dissent harkened back to a pre-Civil War vision of federalism through which the states may act as long as no explicit bar to such actions exists in the Constitution.

Justice Thomas, joined only by his steady judicial partner, Justice Scalia, also dissented in two landmark sexual-harassment cases that the

Court handed down on the last day of its 1997-98 Term. In *Faragher v. City of Boca Raton* and *Burlington Industries, Inc. v. Ellerth*, a seven-person majority developed a rule that employers are vicariously liable if supervisors create a sexually hostile work environment, subject to an affirmative defense by the employer. Justice Thomas's dissent asserted that an employer should be liable for sexual or racial harassment only if the plaintiff proves that the employer was negligent in permitting the supervisor's conduct to occur.

Thomas condemns what he calls the "intellectual slavery" that he asserts liberal black interest groups attempt to impose on him,[11] and he vows to stay on the Court for a long time. Just turning fifty-one in 1999, and the youngest member of the Court in the 1990s, he could remain on the bench well into the twenty-first century. Despite the controversy that continues to haunt his position on the high tribunal, he has come to view it not just as a job, but as a part of his life itself. Requiring only three or four hours of sleep a night, he rises at 4:00 a.m. each day and tries to arrive at his chambers by 7:00 or 7:30. In 1997 he commented movingly, "For one who thought he lost his vocation when he left the seminary, now I know I did not. This is my vocation."[12] This reassessment of his life's work coincided with his reconversion to Roman Catholicism. Although he and his wife had attended an Episcopalian church for many years, he announced at a Holy Cross reunion in 1996 that he had returned to the religion in which his grandparents had raised him. Thomas, who says he "failed" at becoming a priest, now attends daily mass (with his law clerks if they are Catholic). He continues to be inspired by his late grandfather and displays a bust of him in his chambers; the sculpture bears the inscription, "Old Man Can't is dead. I buried him myself."

Justice Thomas may be right about the inevitable failures of those who try to characterize his multilayered life. Critics have indeed portrayed him as a devil, yet among Court employees he is a beloved individual, known for his genuine concern for others and a booming, hearty laugh. He loves cigars and basketball, playing the latter on the "Court's court" until an Achilles tendon injury forced him to the sidelines. Attempting to carry on the mentoring legacy of his grandparents, he and his wife took custody of his six-year-old grandnephew (Thomas's sister's grandson) in 1997 and are raising him in their home in northern Virginia. Justice Thomas has advised audiences, "You must be able to look yourself in the mirror and like what you see." Only he truly knows the meaning of his own image.

ENDNOTES

1. Clarence Thomas, "Commencement Address," *Syracuse Law Review* 42 (1991): 815.

2. Ibid., 820.

3. Remarks televised on *America and the Courts*, C-SPAN, June 17, 1995.

4. See the perceptive and sophisticated analysis of Clarence Thomas's so-called "natural rights" jurisprudence in Scott D. Gerber, "The Jurisprudence of Clarence Thomas," *Journal of Law and Politics* 8 (Fall 1991): 107–41.

5. Qtd. in Barbara A. Perry and Henry J. Abraham, "A 'Representative' Supreme Court? The Thomas, Ginsburg, and Breyer Appointments," *Judicature* 81 (January/February 1998): 160.

6. Qtd. in Jeff Franks, "Justice Thomas Still Healing From 'Whipping' on Hill," *Washington Post*, February 13, 1998, p. A9.

7. See Karen Testa, "Justice Thomas Offers Advice in Visit With Schoolchildren," *Washington Post*, December 21, 1997, p. A4.

8. Qtd. in Joseph Neff, "Thomas Stands Firm in His Beliefs," *Raleigh News and Observer*, November 1994, p. 3A.

9. 515 U.S. 70 (1995).

10. Perry and Abraham, p. 161.

11. Thomas delivered a bitter, blistering counter-attack against such attempts to have him tow the liberal line of many African Americans at a meeting of the National Bar Association in Memphis, Tennessee on July 29, 1998.

12. Qtd. in Testa, p. A4.

CHAPTER EIGHT

Ruth Bader Ginsburg

"A woman, a mother, a Jew—the kiss of death."[1] With that pithy observation, a friend of Ruth Ginsburg described the very essence of only the second woman ever to serve on the Supreme Court of the United States. As a female, Ginsburg has championed the cause of women's rights both on and off the Court. As a mother, she proudly proclaims the achievements of her children and grandchildren. As a Jew, she has cited "the demand for justice [that] runs through the entirety of the Jewish tradition,"[2] and she has pledged to serve that demand. Yet each characteristic of her essence constituted a professional obstacle, and cumulatively they posed severe handicaps in her early career. That she rose above gender and religious discrimination to achieve such demonstrable success is a tribute to her intellect, perseverance, and character.

Born on March 15, 1933, in Brooklyn, New York, Joan Ruth Bader was the second child of Nathan and Celia Bader. Her older sister died several years later, and young Ruth's parents pinned all their hopes on her. Most girls in the Baders' ethnic neighborhood were expected to marry professional men in order to have a comfortable life, but Ruth's mother taught her to be independent and began saving money for her college tuition.

Ruth Bader's talents and interests emerged early in her education. She graduated first in her class from New York's P.S. 238, where she had written a school newspaper article entitled "Landmarks of Constitutional Freedom." Appropriately for her interest in constitutional history and her future career path, Ruth attended James Madison High School, named for the "Father of the Constitution." By all accounts, she was a popular, studious, and competitive student there. In a senior class from which virtually everyone was college-bound, Ruth graduated sixth, with her highest marks in English. Sadly, the day before her high-school commencement, Ruth's beloved mother—her constant source of inspiration—succumbed to cancer.

Although her mother's carefully saved nest egg totaled $8,000, Ruth gave most of the money to her widowed father and enrolled in Cornell as a scholarship student. At the campus in upstate New York, Bader was a serious student but also enjoyed an active social life. She met Marty Ginsburg on a blind date during her freshman year and they became fast friends. On Ruth's way to graduating first in her class, one of her favorite courses was constitutional law. When she and Marty Ginsburg decided that their friendship had blossomed into romance and began to make plans for the future, they determined that law would be a professional field they could both share. Marty, one year older than Ruth, enrolled at Harvard Law School. They were married in 1954 at the end of Ruth's undergraduate career, which was capped by her election to Phi Beta Kappa.

After Marty's two-year stint in the Army and the birth of their first child, Jane, in 1955, the Ginsburgs resettled at Harvard Law School—this time with Ruth entering the first-year class as one of only nine women. She compiled a stellar record at Harvard and earned a coveted spot on the *Law Review*, despite caring for Jane and nursing Marty through a potentially fatal case of testicular cancer. With Ruth auditing his classes and typing his papers, Marty overcame his illness, graduated on time, and received an offer from a law firm in New York City.

Ruth insisted on keeping the family together and chose to forgo her final year at Harvard. She transferred to Columbia Law School, where she was one of only twelve women in the 353-member class of 1959. At their thirty-fifth reunion, Justice Ginsburg met with her female compatriots and recalled the discrimination they had faced. The women remembered being asked why they were taking a man's place in law school. Justice Ginsburg recollected an incident when a law professor argued that married women were like dogs because men were masters over both. The future justice graduated from Columbia first in her class and earned a spot on another Ivy League law review.

Yet, like her future colleague Sandra Day O'Connor, Ginsburg found the doors of private law firms closed to her. Her credentials meant nothing in light of her gender, marital and maternal status, and religious affiliation. Finally, an open-minded U.S. District Court Judge, Edmund L. Palmieri, hired her as his law clerk. After her clerkship, one of her former professors from Columbia asked if she would like to accept a research position in Sweden to write a book on that country's legal system. Intrigued by the opportunity to live abroad for several months and the chance to see her own ideas between the covers of a book, she readily accepted the opportunity.

When Ginsburg returned to the states, Rutgers Law School offered her a teaching position. Her acceptance made her only the second female on the school's faculty and one of the first twenty women law professors in the country. She continued teaching throughout her pregnancy with son James in 1965, hiding her condition under baggy clothes so as not to disrupt her march toward tenure. Shortly thereafter students asked Ginsburg to offer a course on feminist law, and she discovered a dearth of materials on the subject.

Ginsburg could not have imagined that someday she would make such seminal contributions to what is now viewed as the core of landmark gender equity cases. Yet by the early 1970s she knew the legal landscape had to change for women. The final straw for Ginsburg had been the 1961 U.S. Supreme Court decision in *Hoyt v. Florida*. A battered and abused wife, Mrs. Hoyt, had been convicted by an all-male jury of beating her husband to death with a baseball bat. Florida law included only men in calls for jury duty; women could serve but only if they volunteered for jury service. The Supreme Court's ruling implied that women should feel honored that Florida law recognized the "peculiar characteristics, destiny, and mission of women" that compelled them to be wives and mothers. (And this was from the liberal Warren Court that had so generously interpreted civil rights for blacks.) A vivid metaphor from the pen of a California Supreme Court justice in a 1971 case would resonate with Ginsburg as a counter to the outdated reasoning of the *Hoyt* decision. The California Court had written: "The pedestal upon which women have been placed has all too often, upon closer inspection, been revealed as a cage."[3]

Ginsburg had the opportunity to borrow the California Court's eloquence and rationale in her capacity as founder and leader of the Women's Rights Project of the American Civil Liberties Union in 1971. The U.S. Supreme Court had consistently upheld laws with gender classifications if the government merely could prove a "rational relation" between the classification and the government's legislative goal. Ginsburg developed a brilliant strategy to move the Court gradually away from its previous interpretation of the Fourteenth Amendment's Equal Protection Clause in gender cases. In 1971 she took her first case, *Reed v. Reed*, to the Supreme Court, and the future justice has admitted that she did not know if she could keep her breakfast down that morning when she stepped to the imposing rostrum before the nine men on the highest court in the land. Then she realized that they had to listen to her for the time allotted each side in oral argument, and she overcame a nervous stomach to present her position.

Breaking new ground in gender jurisprudence, the Supreme Court accepted Ginsburg's argument against an Idaho law that required the state to prefer males to females in disputes over who was entitled to administer a will. Viewing such a law as arbitrary and therefore contrary to the Equal Protection Clause, in *Reed* the Supreme Court for the first time held a statute unconstitutional on the grounds that it discriminated against women.

Between 1971 and 1978 Ginsburg argued six precedent-setting cases before the Supreme Court, winning all but one. Most important for women's rights and gender equity in general (Ginsburg brought some of her cases on behalf of *men* who were being denied equal treatment under the law) was that a majority of the justices eventually accepted her argument that gender classifications in laws should be subjected by the courts to a higher level of scrutiny than the rational-relation test required. Because of Ginsburg's efforts, the judiciary began to apply a heightened scrutiny to gender classifications and required that the state prove an *important* (not just a rational) relation between the gender distinction and the state interest.

In the meantime, Ginsburg had become the first woman hired with tenure at the Columbia Law School in 1972. (Her daughter Jane eventually accepted a chaired professorship there.) Seven years later President Jimmy Carter, determined to add more women and minorities to the federal judiciary, nominated Ruth Ginsburg for a judgeship on the prestigious U.S. Court of Appeals for the District of Columbia, a traditional training ground for Supreme Court justices. In her thirteen years on that visible bench, she compiled a restrained and moderate, yet distinguished, record.

President Bill Clinton, like his Democratic predecessor Jimmy Carter, vowed to increase the "representativeness" of the federal judiciary by nominating qualified female and minority lawyers to judgeships. Criticism of this policy, however, initially persuaded Clinton to search for a white male when presented with his first opportunity to nominate a member of the Supreme Court following Justice Byron White's retirement announcement in March 1993.[4] Clinton had specified to his advisers that he was also looking for a nominee with a "big heart," presumably to counter the Court's "small-hearted" conservatives. To this end, he announced that he would prefer a politician, rather than a sitting judge, in hopes that such a person would be a natural leader who could encourage the Court's emerging center faction (composed of Justices Sandra O'Connor, Anthony Kennedy, and David Souter) to move further left. Three potential nominees seemed to fit the criterion: New York's Governor Mario Cuomo, Secretary of Education Richard Riley, and Interior Secretary Bruce Babbitt. For a variety of reasons, none of the trio worked out, and Clinton lost hope of finding a politician for the Supreme Court.

Nearly three months had passed since White's announced retirement when Clinton turned to a completely different type of nominee: Stephen Breyer, the chief judge of the U.S. Court of Appeals for the First Circuit in Boston. Breyer, who possessed a superb academic and professional record (including a Supreme Court clerkship for Justice Arthur Goldberg), had the advantage of being relatively moderate and was popular among both Republicans and Democrats in the Senate because of his previous service as counsel to the Senate Judiciary Committee. Yet Breyer had a public-relations problem stemming from his failure to pay social security taxes for his part-time cook. Moreover, Breyer, who had just been released from the hospital after a cycling accident, apparently had an awkward luncheon interview with the president. Clinton later told aides that he thought Breyer was selling himself too hard, that his legal interests were too narrow, and that he did not have a "big heart."[5]

As a fallback in case the Breyer nomination did not materialize, Clinton's White House Counsel Bernard Nussbaum had added Ruth Bader Ginsburg to the list of possible nominees. She catapulted to the top of the president's list after an hour-and-a-half meeting with him, during which Clinton "fell in love" with her life's narrative of surviving family tragedies and overcoming personal and professional discrimination.[6]

In announcing her nomination in a Rose Garden ceremony, President Clinton offered three reasons for his selection of Ginsburg: first, her distinguished thirteen-year career on the U.S. Court of Appeals; second, her towering efforts on behalf of women's issues, which made her "to the women's movement what Thurgood Marshall was to the movement for the rights of African Americans"; and third, her proven ability as a consensus builder, as a healer, as a "moderate."[7] Ginsburg's elegant and eloquent acceptance speech, in which she paid tribute to her late mother, moved Clinton to tears, and he excoriated ABC correspondent Brit Hume afterwards when the reporter queried the president about the "zigzag quality" of the selection process that had produced Ginsburg.

Despite Ginsburg's seemingly impeccable feminist credentials, some women's groups did not immediately embrace her nomination. While feminism had evolved in a more radical direction, Ginsburg had grown increasingly centrist during her tenure on the circuit court bench. Although supportive of the outcome in *Roe v. Wade*, she had questioned the rationale behind and the breadth of Justice Harry Blackmun's majority opinion in a speech at New York University Law School two months before her nomination. She remained clearly pro-choice, but abortion rights advocates, such as Kate Michaelman, president of the National Abortion Rights Action League, commented after Ginsburg's nomination that NARAL would monitor her confirmation hearings carefully to determine whether she "will protect a women's fundamental right to privacy." Despite such doubts, the co-president of the National Women's Law Center, Marcia Greenberger, asserted that "Ruth Ginsburg was as responsible as any one person for legal advances that women made under the Equal Protection Clause of the Constitution. As a result, doors of opportunity have been opened that have benefited not only the women themselves but their families."[8]

The Senate had virtually no doubts about Ginsburg's qualifications for her promotion to the Supreme Court. The Senate Judiciary Committee approved her nomination by a vote of 18–0, and the full Senate followed suit by a 96–3 margin in August 1993. With proud husband Marty Ginsburg holding the Bible, Chief Justice William Rehnquist swore Ruth Bader Ginsburg in as the 107th justice of the Supreme Court in a White House ceremony on August 10, 1993.

Justice Ginsburg's initial terms on the high court demonstrated her normally left-of-center pragmatism that Clinton had described in his Rose Garden nomination. She has voted most frequently with liberal Justices David Souter and John Paul Stevens, and with her pragmatic, centrist colleague Justice Breyer, who in 1994 became Clinton's second nominee to the Supreme Court. Conversely, she infrequently aligns with the conservative wing of the Court, consisting of Chief Justice William Rehnquist and Justices Antonin Scalia and Clarence Thomas.

In civil rights and liberties cases that address gender, race, or religion, Ginsburg can most often be found on the side of the individual or group claiming a violation of rights. Her most visible opinion came in the 1996 *VMI* decision (*United States v. Virginia*) in which she determined for a 7–1 majority (Thomas having recused himself because his son was a cadet there) that state-funded Virginia Military Institute's exclusion of women from its corps of cadets was unconstitutional. Although Ginsburg's opinion for the Court did not boost gender into the highest category of equal-protection analysis—namely, "suspect classification"—where the state must prove a "compelling" interest in order to treat genders differently, she did argue that the government needs an "exceedingly persuasive justification" for any classification based on sex.

In the three important race cases of the 1994–95 term that signaled the Supreme Court's retreat from past precedents favoring minorities, Justice Ginsburg dissented. She questioned the majority's holding in *Adarand v. Peña*, which required that federal affirmative-action plans pass the highest level of equal-protection analysis; took issue with the Court's opinion in *Miller v. Johnson*, which banned the use of race as the predominant criterion in drawing congressional district boundaries; and departed from the majority opinion in *Missouri v. Jenkins II*, which overturned lower court decrees ordering massive expenditures to create integrated magnet schools.

In church and state cases, Justice Ginsburg has hewed to the separationist line preferred by liberals. She joined the Court's five-person majority in the 1994 case of *Board of Education of Kiryas Joel Village v. Grumet* when it held that New York state may not carve out a separate school district to accommodate the special needs of a particular community of "highly religious Satmar Hasidic Jews." In two 1995 cases she dissented from majority rulings that represented to her impermissible mixing of government and religion. They were *Rosenberger v. University of Virginia*, requiring the university to subsidize a student-run Christian magazine through funds collected from the student-activities fee, and *Capitol Square Review Board v. Pinette*, upholding the Ku Klux Klan's erection of a cross on the state capitol grounds in Columbus, Ohio. In addition, she was among the dissenters in the 1997 case *Agostini v. Felton*, which held that public-school teachers may now provide remedial instruction for children *inside* parochial schools under Title I of the Federal Aid to Elementary and Secondary Schools Act of 1965. Her dissenting opinion, however, avoided the broad constitutional arguments of her fellow dissenters and focused on the procedural issues of the case.[9]

In a variety of other cases, ranging from intricate class-action suits to criminal-rights controversies, she has sliced through the complex verbiage of federal and state statutes with the skill and precision of a surgeon. In the 1997 case of *Amchem Products, Inc. v. Windsor*, which arose out of the exceedingly complicated and seemingly endless class action claims of asbestos exposure victims, Ginsburg interpreted Rule 23 of the Federal Rules of Civil Procedure and the Rules Enabling Act as barring "a nationwide administrative claims processing regime." Though she admitted that creating such a regime would "provide the most secure, fair, and efficient means of compensating" asbestos victims, she could not find the latitude to do so in the applicable congressional statutes.

Ginsburg's 1997 opinion for a nearly unanimous Court in *Chandler v. Miller* struck down a Georgia statute requiring candidates for designated state offices to certify that they had taken a urinalysis drug test, with a negative result, within thirty days prior to qualifying for nomination or election. Searching in vain for explicit proof of Georgia's "special need" to overcome Fourth Amendment guarantees against unreasonable search and seizure, Justice Ginsburg declared the state law unconstitutional. One year later she constructed a heated dissent, joined by the unusual alignment of Chief Justice Rehnquist and Justices Scalia and Souter, from the Breyer-authored majority ruling in *Muscarello v. United States*. The Court ruled that Congress's statutory language "uses or carries a firearm" "during and in relation to" a "drug trafficking crime" encompassed a handgun locked in the glove compartment of Muscarello's car, which he used to transport marijuana for sale. Ginsburg, pointedly arguing that unlike the majority she did not have to rely on dictionaries for statutory meaning, urged a narrow definition of "carry" (bear in "such a manner as to be ready for use as a weapon") that could logically be gleaned from the relevant context of the statute.

Although each of these cases garnered headlines, and several will be deemed landmarks long into the future, Justice Ginsburg's reasoning in her opinions has proved much less sweeping than that of paradigmatic liberals like Justices William J. Brennan, Jr., and Thurgood Marshall or Chief Justice Earl Warren, who preceded her on the bench. Her *VMI* decision is illustrative; instead of boosting gender into the "suspect category," requiring a compelling interest from the state in order to classify on the basis of sex, Ginsburg argued that a state must demonstrate an "exceedingly persuasive justification" for using gender-based distinctions. Did she split the difference between "heightened scrutiny" and "strict scrutiny"? Commentators are divided on how to interpret her language, but it is certain that a more activist judge in the Brennan mold would have taken the opportunity to rule broadly by placing gender on a par with race in equal-protection analysis. Moreover, as symbolically meaningful as the *VMI* ruling was, it was substantively applicable only to two schools: the state-run, all-male military academies of Virginia Military Institute and the Citadel. After the decision came down, the media were anxious to speculate on how the opinion would apply to single-gender private colleges or primary and secondary public-school programs that are segregated by gender. Yet the Ginsburg opinion gave no hint of how the Court would rule on those different fact situations. As Ginsburg has commented generally on her approach to drafting rulings for the Court: "I continue to aim for opinions that both get it right, and keep it tight, without undue digressions or decorations or distracting denunciations of colleagues who hold different views."[10]

So in both jurisprudence and personality, Justice Ginsburg is somewhat of a paradox: a pioneer in the feminist revolution of the 1970s but a jurist wedded to the incrementalism of the rule of law; a quiet, reserved, diminutive fixture at the Court's public receptions but a willing, delighted "extra" in period costume on the stage of the Washington Opera; a moderate liberal whose close friend on the Court is archconservative Antonin Scalia because, Ginsburg reports, he makes her laugh. (Scalia, also an opera buff, appeared with her in powdered wig and knee breeches in the production of Richard Strauss's *Ariadne auf Naxos*. A photograph of the two of them together on stage is one of Justice Ginsburg's favorites.)

Ginsburg's demure and deliberate social persona vanishes on the bench, where she is a frequent, incisive, and insistent questioner during oral arguments. Shortly after she arrived at the high court, stories appeared in the media that Justice O'Connor was annoyed that her questions were being interrupted by Ginsburg. When asked about the alleged conflict, Justice Ginsburg explained that she could not always see her colleagues, or determine when they were speaking, from the far end of the bench where by tradition the most junior justice sits. More to the point, she related her amusement that the press never reports male justices interrupting other male justices (which happens quite frequently on this very vocal Court). Justice Ginsburg, however, prefers to accentuate the positive experiences of serving on the Supreme Court, reporting that in private the justices have "heated discussions, lively discussions, but not what one would regard as angry disagreements. This place specializes in reason. We reason together."[11]

Looking back on her unprecedented career, Ginsburg responds bemusedly when asked if it has gone as she planned. With the limited opportunities available to her generation, she literally could not have planned her professional trajectory. And its apogee may still lie in the future: Court observers frequently speculate that she would be a logical choice for the first woman chief justice if the Court's center chair comes vacant during a Democratic presidential administration. If fate allows, she would assume it with all the talent, diligence, and familial support that initially brought her to the "marble palace."

ENDNOTES

1. Qtd. in David Van Drehle, "Brooklyn Melting Pot Forged Future Crusader," *Washington Post,* July 18, 1993, p. A14.
2. Qtd. in "What Being Jewish Means to Me," American Jewish Committee, online at www.ajc.org.
3. Qtd. in Lyle Denniston, "Ruth Bader Ginsburg's Long March to *VMI*," speech at the Annual Spring Law Club Dinner, Baltimore, Md., May 20, 1997.
4. Elizabeth Drew, *On the Edge: The Clinton Presidency* (New York: Simon & Schuster, 1994), chapter 15.
5. Ibid.
6. Ibid.
7. Barbara A. Perry and Henry J. Abraham, "A 'Representative' Supreme Court? The Thomas, Ginsburg, and Breyer Appointments," *Judicature* 81 (January/February 1998): 162–63.
8. Qtd. in Neil A. Lewis, "Rejected As a Clerk, Chosen As a Justice: Ruth Bader Ginsburg," *New York Times*, June 15, 1993, p. A23.
9. See Jeffrey Rosen's fascinating feature on Justice Ginsburg, in which he argues that she is the epitome of the pragmatic, centrist, incremental jurist, "The New Look of Liberalism on the Court," *New York Times Magazine*, October 5, 1997.
10. Ruth Bader Ginsburg, "Remarks for American Law Institute Annual Dinner, May 19, 1994," *Saint Louis University Law Journal* 38 (1994): 887.
11. Remarks televised on *Prime Time Live*, ABC, December 29, 1994.

CHAPTER NINE

Stephen G. Breyer

Shortly after his elevation to the Supreme Court of the United States, Justice Breyer was flying to San Francisco, his birthplace, to speak at a Stanford University alumni event. In the seat next to him was a San Francisco attorney who asked Breyer what he did for a living. The new justice responded modestly that he was "a judge." When the lawyer asked on what court, Breyer stated vaguely "the Supreme Court." And when the persistent passenger questioned at which level, Breyer had to reveal his status and say, "United States." To which the attorney exclaimed, "Oh, you must be Shirley Black's nephew!" referring to Breyer's aunt, who is a well-known labor lawyer in the City by the Bay.[1] The anecdote illustrates the relative anonymity in which members of the U.S. Supreme Court labor. Nevertheless, prior to his promotion to the nation's highest court, Stephen Breyer was well known among his judicial colleagues as a "judge's judge." As a longtime friend put it, "Stephen Breyer is not only the best judge in the United States, but everybody knows it."[2] His Aunt Shirley had always known he would be "something great" because baby Stephen "started speaking in complete sentences."[3]

Breyer's background aptly predicted his success. His father, Irving, was a lawyer and counsel to the San Francisco Board of Education for forty-two years. His mother, Anne, was active in public affairs through the local Democratic Party and the League of Women Voters. Both parents encouraged young Stephen, born August 15, 1938, and his younger brother Charles to participate in the real world as well as the world of ideas. Mr. Breyer enjoyed entertaining his family with colorful stories of the conflicts between political factions in the arena of public education, and Mrs. Breyer's membership in the United Nations Association ensured that an array of international figures streamed through the Breyer household. As was typical of the large middle-class Jewish community in San Francisco, the Breyers put a premium on formal education. Stephen attended a public elementary school and was sent to Lowell High School, known as an academically rigorous public institution, where he excelled, seemingly effortlessly. He won prizes for his performances in math and science, as well as for his debating skills. Prophetically, he was voted "most likely to succeed." True to form, he also achieved the rank of Eagle Scout as a member of the Boy Scouts, though on outings he earned the dubious moniker, "Blister King."

Stephen narrowed his college choices to Harvard and Stanford, and his mother, worried that her elder son would become too isolated and scholarly if he chose Harvard, urged him to select Stanford for its well-rounded approach to education. Like his father, and eventually his own son, Breyer chose to pursue his undergraduate degree at Stanford. His grades there were perfect except for one B (which left him "distraught," in the words of a classmate), and he graduated with "Great Distinction" and a membership in Phi Beta Kappa in 1959. His lack of athletic prowess doomed his attempt to earn a Rhodes Scholarship, but he fulfilled his desire to attend Oxford University by winning a Marshall Scholarship. At Oxford's Magdalen College, he successfully pursued friendships with the British students (no easy feat for an American), and achieved the equally difficult goal of placing in the "First Class" for his degree in politics, philosophy, and economics in 1961.

Despite eschewing Harvard for his undergraduate studies, Breyer returned from England to enroll at Harvard Law School. He thrived on the infamous Socratic method used by Harvard's elite professors to intimidate first-year law students. While most of the students dreaded the thought of being called upon and slouched in their seats to avoid being recognized, Breyer eagerly volunteered to respond to the professors' questions. One classmate from that era remembers thinking about Breyer's intellect and willingness to debate, "This guy will be heard from again."[4]

Some of his research at Harvard concentrated on pragmatism and the law, with Breyer theorizing that judges should determine the social, political, and legal impact of their decisions on the people affected by their outcomes. Once more, Breyer compiled a first-rate record; he was elected to the *Harvard Law Review*, where he served as articles editor, and graduated *magna cum laude* in 1964. In recognition of his stellar performance, Supreme Court Justice Arthur Goldberg invited Breyer to be his law clerk for one year after leaving Harvard Law School. During Breyer's tenure as a clerk in 1964–65, the Supreme Court handed down its landmark decision in *Griswold v. Connecticut*, which invalidated a state law prohibiting the distribution of contraceptives to married couples. The majority opinion, written by Justice William O. Douglas, extrapolated a right to privacy from the "penumbras" and "emanations" of the Bill of Rights, including its Ninth Amendment, which states that "the enumeration in the Constitution, of certain rights, shall not be construed to deny or disparage others retained by the people."[5] Justice Goldberg contributed a concurring opinion, drafted by Breyer, expounding upon the foundation of the Ninth Amendment for discovering rights not explicitly guaranteed in the Constitution's language.

After his clerkship, Breyer remained in Washington as a special assistant to the assistant attorney general in the Antitrust Division of the Department of Justice. During this two-year stint in the nation's capital, he met Joanna Hare, a twenty-four-year-old assistant to the *London Sunday Times* Washington correspondent, at a Georgetown dinner party in 1966. Joanna, the daughter of Lord Blakenham, who once led Britain's Conservative Party and was heir to a British media fortune, had an Oxford degree in politics, philosophy, and economics; Breyer had also studied "PPE" on his Marshall Scholarship to Oxford. In addition, the couple shared a love of bicycling and camping. She admired his wit and intelligence; he enjoyed her lovely demeanor and sharp intellect that was a challenge to his own. In September 1967 they were married in a village church in Suffolk, England. In deference to Breyer's Jewish religion, references to Christ were expunged from the Church of England wedding ceremony.

The newlyweds settled in Cambridge, Massachusetts, where Stephen accepted an assistant professorship at Harvard Law School and Joanna earned a master's degree in education and a doctorate in psychology from Harvard. She gave birth to three children (Chloe in 1969, Nell in 1971, and Michael in 1974) and eventually became a clinical psychologist at the

Dana Farber Cancer Institute in Boston, specializing in juvenile leukemia cases.[6]

Stephen Breyer carved out a niche teaching and researching antitrust issues, administrative law, and economic regulation, and he was promoted to full professor at Harvard in 1970, a position he held until 1980, with several return engagements in Washington for government service. Indeed, his parents would have been proud of his combining the scholarly life with contributions to public affairs. In 1973 Breyer served as an assistant special prosecutor for the Watergate Special Prosecution Force, and in 1974–75 he was special counsel to the Administrative Practices Subcommittee of the U.S. Senate Judiciary Committee. He returned in 1979–80 as the Judiciary Committee's chief counsel. In the last position, he exhibited his skill in bipartisan negotiating, especially in his work on deregulation of the airline industry, which allowed him to embody his pragmatic approach to law and economics. Breyer believes that laws can implement a balance between the freedom of the marketplace and the government regulation necessary to protect consumers. Thus, business and industry are free to be productive and profitable, but not at the expense of and injury to the American people. Airline deregulation produced decidedly mixed results, including lower airfares and bankruptcies of unprofitable carriers. Nevertheless, the policy showcased Breyer's prodigious intellectual and political talents.

The latter stood him in good stead when President Jimmy Carter nominated him for a seat on the U.S. Court of Appeals for the First Circuit at the end of his term in 1980. The change of parties in both the White House and Senate doomed other last-minute Carter nominees, but Breyer received support from Republicans as well as Democrats, ensuring his confirmation. Once on the Court of Appeals, Breyer again displayed his legal pragmatism. His opinions, which he insisted on writing himself without using footnotes (after Justice Goldberg suggested that he drop citations), were noted for their brevity, incisiveness, and ability to persuade the two other members of the typical three-judge panel. Strict adherence to the facts of a case, rather than sweeping conclusions, was the hallmark of Breyer's appellate opinions. In 1985 he began a four-year term on the U.S. Sentencing Commission, where he put his technical expertise to work in overhauling federal criminal sentencing guidelines for judges. He developed a complex grid or template into which judges must plug factors such as the severity of a crime and the defendant's past criminal record. Proponents of the system argue that it standardizes a previously idiosyncratic system, but federal judges complain about the loss of discretion in sentencing decisions. Civil libertarians maintain that it puts a premium on law and order while discriminating against first-time offenders and black males. In a 1989 case, *Mistretta v. United States*, the U.S. Supreme Court upheld the constitutionality of the U.S. Sentencing Commission. Breyer's obvious administrative and consensus-building talents vaulted him into the chief justiceship of the First Circuit in 1990; in that position he planned a stunning new federal courthouse overlooking Boston Harbor. It has earned both kudos and criticism for its opulence.

Not surprisingly, Breyer's judicial record on the Court of Appeals was considered moderately liberal and marked by a continuing interest in antitrust cases, in which he attempted to find the happy medium between business concerns and the public good. His centrist posture dovetailed perfectly with Bill Clinton's own ideology, and the new president seriously considered Breyer for the Supreme Court seat vacated by Justice Byron White's retirement in the spring of 1993. After an unsuccessful attempt at finding a politician with a "big heart" for his first Supreme Court nomination, Clinton turned to Breyer. Leaving his hospital bed, to which he was confined with a punctured lung and broken ribs after a cycling accident, Breyer took the train to Washington, where he was met at Union Station by the ill-fated Associate White House Counsel Vincent Foster (who would commit suicide a few weeks later). Breyer's impeccable credentials could not overcome an awkward luncheon conversation between Clinton and the ailing judge, or the fact that he and his wife had neglected to pay social security taxes for their part-time cook. Such an issue had derailed President Clinton's first nominee for attorney general, Zoe Baird. The President then turned to Judge Ruth Bader Ginsburg of the U.S. Court of Appeals for the District of Columbia, whose nomination to the Supreme Court sailed smoothly through the Senate.

Instead of sulking over his bad luck, Breyer graciously attended Ginsburg's swearing-in ceremony—a cordial gesture not lost on President Clinton. When Justice Harry Blackmun announced his retirement from the Supreme Court the next year, Breyer's name went back on the list of candidates who might succeed him. Clinton still longed to place a politician in the Earl Warren mold on the high court, but Senate Majority Leader George Mitchell, an erstwhile federal judge, declined. Nominating Interior Secretary Bruce Babbitt, the former governor of Arizona, threatened to provoke a Senate battle, which Clinton could ill afford while his proposed health-care-reform bill siphoned off his meager political capital. Clinton leaned toward his longtime Arkansas friend Judge Richard Arnold of the U.S. Court of Appeals for the Eighth Circuit but eventually jettisoned his nomination, fearing charges of cronyism and controversy over Arnold's previous bout with cancer.

Breyer's former boss at the Senate Judiciary Committee, Senator Edward Kennedy (D.-Mass.), lobbied hard for the jurist from his home state. Again attracting bipartisan support, as he had for his initial nomination to the federal bench, Breyer won praise from Senator Orrin Hatch (R.-Utah), who urged President Clinton to nominate him. Noting Breyer's backing from two such diverse partisans, the president did so on May 13, 1994. Although he had debated several weeks over Blackmun's replacement, Clinton was so quick with his announcement once the decision to nominate Breyer was made that the appeals court judge could not travel from Boston to Washington quickly enough to be at the president's side. Instead, a formal appearance for Clinton and Breyer in the White House Rose Garden took place several days after the initial nomination. In offering Breyer's name to the Senate and the American people, the president emphasized that the appellate jurist possessed "a clear grasp of the law, a boundless respect for the constitutional and legal rights of the American people, a searching and restless intellect and a remarkable ability to explain complex subjects in understandable terms."[7] Responding to his selection, Breyer vowed to interpret the law to benefit ordinary people and echoed the American people's faith in the Supreme Court. With his exemplary academic and professional record (he had served in all three branches of government) and his talent for forging consensus, Breyer earned unanimous approval from the Senate Judiciary Committee. He then garnered confirmation from the full Senate by a vote of 87–9 on July 29, 1994, with the opposition led by Richard Lugar (R.-Ind.), who questioned the propriety of several investment ventures Breyer had made, particularly one with Lloyds of London.

The newly confirmed justice would experience three separate swearing-in ceremonies. The first occurred at Chief Justice William Rehnquist's summer home in Vermont on August 3, 1994, so that Breyer could begin to start work and hire his law clerks. Eight days later a more formal ceremony took place at the White House, followed by the Court's public investiture of Breyer just before the opening of its 1994–95 term in October. In Justice Breyer's first weeks on the high bench he distinguished himself as a frequent and professorial questioner at oral argument. Unfailingly polite to counsel in the unenviable position of debating complex questions before the Supreme Court, Breyer often poses multipart queries in a classroom lecture style. Sometimes he pitches his body forward on the bench, leaning on his elbows and cradling his bald head in his hands, as he earnestly attempts to decipher a counsel's response.

Breyer throws himself into his job with a youthful zeal that belies his age. In an interview conducted eight months after he assumed his position on the Supreme Court, he remarked about his new job, "I am very enthusiastic about it. I might find myself here fairly late in the evenings, simply because time is passing quickly and I am finding what I am doing so fascinating."[8] In January 1995 he became so excited in summarizing his first opinion for the Court, in a case that arose out of an extermination company's termite contract, that he forgot to add that there were two dissenting opinions. After he concluded his scholarly synopsis and remained silent, Justice Clarence Thomas, who sits next to Breyer on the bench, and Chief Justice Rehnquist both stage-whispered, "The dissents!" A bit sheepishly, Breyer smiled and replied, "Oh, there was a dissent [actually two] as well."

Justice Breyer occasionally adds a touch of impish wit to the oral argument. In April 1995 the Court heard the case of *Vernonia School District v. Acton*, which raised the question of whether drug-testing (through urinalysis) of middle- and high-school student athletes who have not engaged in suspicious behavior is constitutional. Chief Justice Rehnquist opened the way for some "locker-room humor" with his reasoning that urinalysis is hardly a violation of privacy when boys' locker rooms are rarely private, with their rows of open urinals and "guys walking around naked." Justice Breyer added that he did not think that providing a urine sample was necessarily an intrusion on privacy because urination is a fact of life. Or as the new justice put it (betraying a male perspective), "It isn't really a tremendously private thing." For the record, the attorney for Vernonia student James Acton had to concede that everyone urinates. The lawyer, visibly nervous over this line of questioning on a rather delicate subject, added, "In fact, I might do so here!" With that frank admission-*cum*-quip, which brought a spontaneous eruption of laughter from the audience, he bested Rehnquist and Breyer with some improvised humor of his own. Ultimately, the Court ruled against Acton and in favor of the Vernonia School District's drug-testing policy; Justice Breyer joined the majority in the 6–3 decision.

Yet despite occasional humorous exchanges on the bench, Breyer performs his role on the Supreme Court with the utmost respect for the institution he serves. In June 1995, just eight months after he was sworn in as the 108th justice of the Supreme Court, Breyer presided over the swearing-in ceremony of the new directors of the Holocaust Museum in Washington, D.C. The seventh Jewish member to serve on the high court in its history, Breyer was an obvious choice to read the oath of office for each new director. Standing in the museum's Hall of Remembrance with its eternal flame flickering in the background, Breyer began with a remembrance of his first tour through the museum. Like many others who have taken the several-hour journey through the barbarism that marked the Holocaust, he had been overcome with emotion and rendered speechless after the experience. In addition to an emotional reaction based on his own Jewish background, he was also overcome by thoughts related to his status as a lawyer and a judge. He recalled that there were laws, lawyers, and judges in Nazi Germany, but that they had not prevented—indeed they had sometimes facilitated—the terror and annihilation that marked the horrific reign of Hitler's Third Reich. He noted that Americans often express frustration over the inefficiency of the United States government, but Breyer reminded his audience that their frustration results from the separation of powers, which the Founders designed to curb the kind of unrestrained power that in the twentieth century was exercised by Nazi Germany.

Justice Breyer then spoke of his new job at the Supreme Court in a voice filled with passion and awe. He observed, "I go into this courtroom . . . and I feel this history. This is the room in which *Brown v. Board of Education* was decided. This is the room in which so many things of historic importance have transpired. And the feeling that I get is a feeling of responsibility. I must take part in an institution that has to transmit from the past these traditions and values to the next generation."[9]

Breyer has also spoken movingly of the need to continue the fight against racial, religious, and gender discrimination, noting that his own father was barred from social clubs at Stanford because he was Jewish. Not surprisingly, on the Supreme Court Breyer has championed civil rights and liberties generally (with some notable exceptions in the criminal-rights realm), almost always joining the Stevens-Souter-Ginsburg group on such issues. In his first two terms on the high bench, Breyer most frequently sided with Ginsburg and least frequently with Thomas and Scalia. He voted with the dissenters in the 1995 affirmative-action case *Adarand v. Peña*, which required federal government preferences for minority businesses to meet the highest level of scrutiny, and he also aligned with the minority in the racial gerrymandering cases of 1995 that struck down congressional districts drawn with race as the predominant consideration.

In religion cases Justice Breyer voted on the separationist side (each time in dissent) in the 1995 case requiring the University of Virginia to provide funds from the student-activities fee to a student-sponsored Christian magazine, and in the 1997 New York decision allowing public-school remedial instructors to teach in parochial schools. He sided with the accommodationists, however, in the Columbus, Ohio Ku Klux Klan case, sanctioning that city's public forum, which is open to a variety of private expression, both religious (in this instance a cross erected by the Klan) and nonreligious. He also voted (in dissent) to uphold the Religious

Freedom Restoration Act in 1997 as a valid exercise of Congress's
authority to require the highest level of protection for religious claims
against government regulation.

In two 1996 free-expression cases (*Denver Area Educational
Telecommunications Consortium, Inc. v. Federal Communications
Commission* and *Colorado Republican Federal Campaign Committee v.
Federal Election Commission),* Justice Breyer upheld First Amendment
claims by challengers of regulatory statutes applying to cable television
and campaign financing, respectively. Television viewers in the Denver
case had challenged portions of the Cable Television Consumer Protection
and Competition Act of 1992, as implemented by the FCC. Breyer's
opinion for the Court struck down the Act's provision that required
operators of leased access channels to segregate "patently offensive"
programming on a single channel, to block that channel from viewer
access, and to unblock it (or later reblock it) within thirty days of a
subscriber's written request. Breyer reasoned that such a requirement was
overly restrictive and its benefits speculative. Likewise, he upheld the
right of the Federal Campaign Committee (Colorado Party) to fund,
independently of any GOP candidate, radio advertisements attacking the
Democratic Party's likely candidate. Dollar limits imposed by the Federal
Election Campaign Act of 1971 on such activities were an unconstitutional
violation of the First Amendment, argued Breyer in his opinion for the
Court.

Justice Breyer's most visible opinion thus far was his lead dissent in
the 1995 landmark *U.S. v. Lopez* case, in which the 5–4 majority
invalidated the Gun-Free School Zones Act of 1990 on the grounds that
it had exceeded Congress's authority to regulate interstate commerce.
Applying his economic reasoning to the dispute, Breyer argued that if
Congress found that guns disrupted schools to such an extent as to affect
education's impact on interstate and foreign commerce, the legislature was
well within its constitutional purview to implement a gun-free school zone
policy. He also dissented in the 1997 Brady Act case, which invalidated
the portion of the *national* gun-control act that required *state* law-
enforcement authorities to maintain records of gun purchases. Whereas
the Court's majority found the statute's requirement to be a violation of

federalism, Breyer argued in his dissent that "there is no need to interpret the Constitution as containing an absolute principle—forbidding the assignment of virtually any federal duty to any state officer."[10]

Breyer added to this pattern of broadly reading law-enforcement statutes through his majority opinion in *Muscarello v. United States*. At issue was the federal law that adds five years to the prison sentence of anyone who carries a firearm while trafficking in illegal drugs. Muscarello transported marijuana for sale in his truck, where law-enforcement officials also found a handgun in the locked glove compartment. The Supreme Court ruled that the gun was "carried" within the meaning of the statute and therefore triggered the additional five-year sanction. Breyer's opinion for the five-justice majority was joined by the unusual alignment of Justices John Paul Stevens, Sandra Day O'Connor, Anthony Kennedy, and Clarence Thomas.

In hindsight, Breyer's concurrence in *Clinton v. Jones*, which almost read like a dissent, was prescient. The Court unanimously decided in 1997 that Paula Jones's civil suit against President Clinton for alleged sexual harassment could go forward, even during his White House tenure. Breyer warned in his concurring opinion that such litigation could prove highly distracting to an incumbent president. Although the trial court judge eventually dismissed the Jones case for insufficient evidence (and while it was still on appeal, Clinton settled), Special Prosecutor Kenneth Starr's collateral investigation of White House intern Monica Lewinsky's affair with President Clinton did indeed prove distracting and embarrassing for the nation's chief executive. It ultimately led to his impeachment by the House of Representatives in 1998; the Senate, however, acquitted Clinton in early 1999 after a trial presided over by Chief Justice Rehnquist.

Not surprisingly, given Justice Breyer's broad experience in economic regulation and administrative law, he has written a number of cases involving business practices. Indeed, his first opinion for the Court in *Allied Bruce Terminix Cos., Inc. v. Dobson* (the aforementioned termite extermination contract case) contained his broad interpretation of Section 2 of the Federal Arbitration Act under Congress's Commerce Clause power, in order to preclude a state from applying an antiarbitration policy.

The Dobsons had sued the exterminating company after an inspection of their new home, covered by a Terminix contract, revealed a termite infestation. In *Qualitex Co. v. Jacobson Products, Co., Inc.*, Justice Breyer wrote for a unanimous Court that the Lanham Trademark Act of 1946 "permits the registration of a trademark that consists, purely and simply, of a color." Qualitex, manufacturers of dry-cleaning press pads with a distinctive green-gold coloring, had brought suit against their rival, Jacobson Products, for making similarly colored pads.

The bulk of Breyer's record on the high bench still lies in the future. Nevertheless, he has compiled a record that coheres with his previous work on the U.S. Court of Appeals and his scholarly interests in economic regulation and administrative law. Even while on the Supreme Court he has continued to teach at Harvard, contributing approximately ten sessions each year to a seminar on business regulation and administrative law at the John F. Kennedy School of Government. He has commented that he finds it "refreshing and invigorating" to meet directly with students, from whom he continues to learn in the academic fields that interest him. Moreover, Justice Breyer maintains that teaching is "a way of escaping some of the isolating features" of life in the "marble palace."[11]

Although critics sometimes describe Breyer as cool and aloof, he can display a genuine interest in others. And he continues to embrace life's challenges with the enthusiasm and determination that marked his youth. In his fifties, he took up Spanish, teaching himself the language through tapes that he listened to during his morning exercise routine, and practicing his newfound skill with Spanish-speaking dignitaries who visit the Supreme Court. He still enjoys cycling despite his harrowing 1993 accident, when a car plowed into him as he pedaled through Harvard Yard. But primarily he seems truly to relish the life and work of a judge at the pinnacle of his profession. He argues that all the work of the jurist (unlike that of the legislator) is displayed in the written fruits of his labors—the legal opinions. As Justice Breyer is fond of saying, "The inside story of the Court is that there is no inside story." Although journalists and academics alike would disagree with that conclusion, Breyer's devotion to his craft of judging is indeed inspiring.

ENDNOTES

1. See "Fleeting Fame," *Legal Times*, December 5, 1994, p. 3.
2. Qtd. in Joan Biskupic, "A Judicial Pragmatist," *Washington Post*, May 14, 1994, p. A1.
3. Qtd. in Malcolm Gladwell, "Judge Breyer's Life Fashioned Like His Courthouse," *Washington Post*, June 26, 1994, p. A18.
4. Ibid.
5. 381 U.S. 479.
6. See Lloyd Grove's "The Courtship of Joanna Breyer," *Washington Post*, July 11, 1994, p. B1, for a delightful account of the Breyers' successful partnership.
7. Qtd. in "Excerpts From Clinton's Remarks Announcing His Selection for Top Court, *New York Times*, May 14, 1994, p. A10.
8. Interview with Stephen Breyer, *Docket Sheet of the Supreme Court of the United States* 31 (Summer 1995): 3.
9. Remarks televised on *America and the Courts*, C-SPAN, June 24, 1995.
10. *Printz v. U.S.*, 65 LW 4731.
11. Interview with Stephen Breyer, *Docket Sheet*, 12.

BIBLIOGRAPHY

GENERAL SOURCES ON SUPREME COURT JUSTICES

Abraham, Henry J. *Justices, Presidents, and Senators: A History of Appointments to the Supreme Court*. 4th ed. Lanham, Md.: Rowman & Littlefield, 1999.

Biskupic, Joan, and Elder Witt. *Guide to the U.S. Supreme Court*. Vols. 1, 2. Washington, D.C.: Congressional Quarterly, 1997.

Cornell University. *Supreme Court Collection*. Online. www.supct.law. cornell.edu.

C-SPAN. *America and the Courts*. Online. www.c-span.org.

Cushman, Clare, ed. *The Supreme Court Justices: Illustrated Biographies, 1789–95*. 2d ed. Washington, D.C.: Congressional Quarterly, 1995.

Epstein, Lee, and Jack Knight. *The Choices Justices Make*. Washington, D. C.: Congressional Quarterly, 1998.

Friedman, Leon, and Fred L. Israel, ed. *The Justices of the United States Supreme Court: Their Lives and Major Opinions*. Vols. 1–5. New York: Chelsea House, 1995.

Pederson, William, and Norman Provizer, ed. *Great Justices of the Supreme Court*. New York: Peter Lang, 1992.

Perry, Barbara A., and Henry J. Abraham. "A 'Representative' Supreme Court? The Thomas, Ginsburg, and Breyer Appointments." *Judicature* 81 (January/February 1998): 158–65.

Urofsky, Melvin I., ed. *The Supreme Court Justices: A Biographical Dictionary*. New York: Garland, 1994.

Yalof, David A. *Pursuit of Justices: Presidential Politics and the Selection of Supreme Court Nominees*. Chicago: University of Chicago Press, 1999.

SOURCES ON CURRENT JUSTICES

Stephen G. Breyer:

Biskupic, Joan. "A Judicial Pragmatist." *Washington Post*, May 14, 1994, p. A1.

Farrell, John Aloysius. "Scales of Justice." *Boston Globe Magazine*, May 10, 1998, pp. 16–26+.

Gladwell, Malcolm. "Judge Breyer's Life Fashioned Like His Courthouse." *Washington Post*, June 26, 1994, p. A18.

Ruth Bader Ginsburg:

Ginsburg, Ruth Bader. "Remarks for American Law Institute Annual Dinner, May 19, 1994." *Saint Louis University Law Journal* 38 (1994): 881–88.

Lewis, Neil A. "Rejected As a Clerk, Chosen As a Justice: Ruth Bader Ginsburg." *New York Times*, June 15, 1993, p. A23.

Perry, Barbara A. "Ruth Bader Ginsburg." *Encyclopedia of World Biography*, Vol. 18. Palatine, Il.: Publishers Guild, 1995. 126–27.

Rosen, Jeffrey. "The New Look of Liberalism on the Court." *New York Times Magazine*, October 5, 1997.

Van Drehle, David. "Brooklyn Melting Pot Forged Future Crusader." *Washington Post*, July 18, 1993, p. A14.

Anthony M. Kennedy:

"Anthony M. Kennedy." *1988 Current Biography Yearbook*. New York: Wilson, 1988. 289–92.

Cohodas, Nadine. "Kennedy Finds Bork an Easy Act to Follow." *Congressional Quarterly Weekly Report* 45 (1987): 2989.

Perry, Barbara A. "Anthony M. Kennedy." *Encyclopedia of World Biography*, Vol. 17. Palatine, Il.: Publishers Guild, 1992. 308–09.

_____. "The Life and Death of the 'Catholic Seat' on the United States Supreme Court." *Journal of Law and Politics* 6 (Fall 1989): 55–92.

"Reagan Nominates Kennedy to Fill Court Seat." *Congressional Quarterly Weekly Report* 45 (1987): 2830.

Rosen, Jeffrey. "The Agonizer." *New Yorker*. November 11, 1996, pp. 82-90.

Sandra Day O'Connor:

Cordray, Richard, and James Vrodelis, "The Emerging Jurisprudence of Justice O'Connor." *University of Chicago Law Review* 52 (Spring 1985): 389–459.

Gabor, Andrea. "Sandra Day O'Connor." In *Einstein's Wife: Work and Marriage in the Lives of Five Great Twentieth-Century Women*. New York: Penguin Books, 1995.

"The Jurisprudence of Justice Sandra Day O'Connor." *Women's Rights Law Reporter* 13 (Summer/Fall 1991).

Marie, Joan S. "Her Honor: The Rancher's Daughter." *Saturday Evening Post*, September 1985, pp. 42–47+.

Maveety, Nancy. *Justice Sandra Day O'Connor: Strategist on the Supreme Court*. Lanham, Md.: Rowman & Littlefield, 1996.

Scheb, John M. II, and Lee W. Ailshie, "Justice Sandra Day O'Connor and the 'Freshman Effect.'" *Judicature* 69 (June/July 1985): 10–11.

William H. Rehnquist:

Boles, Donald Edward. *Mr. Justice Rehnquist, Judicial Activist: The Early Years*. Ames: Iowa State University Press, 1987.

Davis, Sue. *Justice Rehnquist and the Constitution*. Princeton, N.J.: Princeton University Press, 1989.

Garrow, David J. "The Rehnquist Years." *New York Times Magazine*, October 6, 1996, pp. 65–71+.

Kleven, Thomas. "The Constitutional Philosophy of Justice William H. Rehnquist." *Vermont Law Review* 8 (Spring 1983): 1-54.

Lardner, George, Jr., and Saundra Saperstein. "Chief Justice-Designate Sought to Redirect U.S." *Washington Post*, July 6, 1986, p. A12.

Rehnquist, William H. *All the Laws But One: Civil Liberties in Wartime*. New York: Knopf, 1998.

_____. *Grand Inquest: The Historic Impeachments of Justice Samuel Chase and President Andrew Johnson*. New York: Morrow, 1992.

_____. "Remarks on the Process of Judging." *Washington and Lee Law Review* 49 (Spring 1992): 263–70.

_____. *The Supreme Court: How It Was, How It Is*. New York: Quill, 1987.

_____. *The Supreme Court*. New Edition. New York: Knopf, 2001.

Antonin Scalia:

Brisbin, Richard A., Jr. "The Conservatism of Antonin Scalia." *Political Science Quarterly* 105 (Spring 1990): 1-29.

_____. *Justice Antonin Scalia and the Conservative Revival*. Baltimore: Johns Hopkins University Press, 1997.

Edelman, Peter B. "Justice Scalia's Jurisprudence and the Good Society: Shades of Felix Frankfurter and the Harvard Hit Parade of the 1950s." *Cardozo Law Review* 12 (June 1991): 1799-1815.

Kannar, George. "The Constitutional Catechism of Antonin Scalia." *Yale Law Journal* 99 (April 1990): 1297–1357.

Kozinski, Alex. "My Pizza With Nino." *Cardozo Law Review* 12 (June 1991): 1583–91.

Marcus, Ruth, and Susan Schmidt. "Scalia Tenacious After Staking Out a Position." *Washington Post*, June 22, 1986, p. A16.

Molotsky, Irvin. "Judge With Tenacity and Charm." *New York Times*, June 18, 1986, p. A31.

Perry, Barbara A. "The Life and Death of the 'Catholic Seat' on the United States Supreme Court." *Journal of Law and Politics* 6 (Fall 1989): 55–92.

Scalia, Antonin. *A Matter of Interpretation: Federal Courts and the Law*. Princeton, N.J.: Princeton University Press, 1997.

Schultz, David A., and Christopher E. Smith. *The Jurisprudential Vision of Justice Antonin Scalia*. Lanham, Md.: Rowman & Littlefield, 1996.

David H. Souter:

Farrell, John Aloysius. "Scales of Justice." *Boston Globe Magazine*, May 10, 1998, pp. 16–26+.

Garrow, David J. "Justice Souter: A Surprising Kind of Conservative." *New York Times Magazine,* September 6, 1994, pp. 36–43+.

Johnson, Scott P., and Christopher E. Smith. "David Souter's First Term on the Supreme Court: The Impact of a New Justice." *Judicature* 75 (February/March): 238–43.

Perry, Barbara A. "David H. Souter." *Encyclopedia of World Biography*. Vol. 17. Palatine, Il.: Publishers Guild, 1992. 512–14.

Rosen, Jeffrey. "The Education of David Souter." (Louisville) *Courier-Journal*, March 21, 1993, pp. D1, D4.

Savage, David G. "Justice Souter: Quiet Scholar Is Forging New Coalition on the Court." (Louisville) *Courier-Journal*, July 10, 1994, p. D1.

Souter, David H. "In Memoriam: William J. Brennan, Jr." *Harvard Law Review* 111 (November 1997): 1.

John Paul Stevens:

Biskupic, Joan. "At Long Last, Seniority: 'Quirky' Stevens Takes Helm of Court's Liberal Wing." *Washington Post*, March 20, 1995, p. A15.

O'Brien, David M. "Filling Justice William O. Douglas's Seat: President Gerald R. Ford's Appointment of Justice John Paul Stevens." *Supreme Court Historical Society Yearbook, 1989*. Washington, D.C.: Supreme Court Historical Society, 1989. 20–39.

Sickels, Robert Judd. *John Paul Stevens and the Constitution: The Search for Balance*. University Park, Pa.: Pennsylvania State University Press, 1988.

Stevens, John Paul. "The Supreme Court of the United States: Reflections After a Summer Recess." *South Texas Law Review* 27 (1986): 447–53.

Rich, Spencer. "Ford Picks Chicago Jurist." *Washington Post*, November 29, 1975, pp. A1, A4.

Clarence Thomas:

Gerber, Scott D. *First Principles: The Jurisprudence of Clarence Thomas*. New York: New York University Press, 1999.

_____. "The Jurisprudence of Clarence Thomas." *Journal of Law and Politics* 8 (Fall 1991): 107–41.

McCaughey, Elizabeth P. "Clarence Thomas's Record as a Judge." *Presidential Studies Quarterly* 21 (Fall 1991): 833–35.

Perry, Barbara A. "Clarence Thomas." *Encyclopedia of World Biography*. Vol. 18. Palatine, Il.: Publishers Guild, 1995. 347–49.

"Politics, Values, and the Thomas Nomination." Symposium in *PS: Political Science and Politics* 25 (September 1992): 473–95.

Thomas, Clarence. "Commencement Address." *Syracuse Law Review* 42 (1991): 815–22.

INDEX

A

Abortion issues, 5-6, 22, 32-33, 46-47, 61, 95. See also *Planned Parenthood of Southeastern Pennsylvania v. Casey*; *Roe v. Wade*; *Wesbster v. Reproductive Health Services*

Acton case, 68, 133-34

Adams, Arlin M., 30

Adarand v. Peña (515 U.S. 200), 22, 34, 51, 66, 82, 98, 109, 121-22

Affirmative action cases, 6, 15-16, 22, 33, 51, 61, 79, 121-22

AFSCME v. State of Washington (770 F.2d 1401), 76

Agostini v. Felton (117 S.Ct. 1997), 52, 122

Akron v. Akron Center for Reproductive Health, Inc. (462 U.S. 416), 50

Allegheny County v. Greater Pittsburgh A.C.L.U. (497 U.S. 573), 79

Allen v. Wright (468 U.S. 757) 48-49

Allied Bruce Terminix Cos., Inc. v. Dobson (513 U.S. 265), 137-38

Amchem Products, Inc. v. Windsor (521 U.S. 591), 122

American Bar Association (ABA), 30-31, 47

Anderson, Christine, 101-2, 111

Anderson, Myers, 68

Arizona v. Hicks (476 U.S. 1156), 68

Arizona v. Norris (463 U.S. 1073), 49

Arnold, Richard, 12

Asbestos exposure cases, 122

B

Babbitt, Bruce, 45, 119, 132

Bader, Nathan and Celia, 115-16

Baker, Howard, 13

Bakke case, 16, 33

Bavarian Motor Works (BMW) v. Gore (517 U.S. 559), 37

Beller v. Middendorf (632 F.2d 788), 76

Black, Shirley, 127

Index

Teaching Texts in Law and Politics

David Schultz, *General Editor*

The new series Teaching Texts in Law and Politics is devoted to textbooks that explore the multidimensional and multidisciplinary areas of law and politics. Special emphasis will be given to textbooks written for the undergraduate classroom. Subject matters to be addressed in this series include, but will not be limited to: constitutional law; civil rights and liberties issues; law, race, gender, and gender orientation studies; law and ethics; women and the law; judicial behavior and decision-making; legal theory; comparative legal systems; criminal justice; courts and the political process; and other topics on the law and the political process that would be of interest to undergraduate curriculum and education. Submission of single-author and collaborative studies, as well as collections of essays are invited.

Authors wishing to have works considered for this series should contact:

> Peter Lang Publishing
> Acquisitions Department
> 275 Seventh Avenue, 28th floor
> New York, New York 10001

To order other books in this series, please contact our Customer Service Department at:

> 800-770-LANG (within the U.S.)
> (212) 647-7706 (outside the U.S.)
> (212) 647-7707 FAX

or browse online by series at:

> WWW.PETERLANGUSA.COM